Database Anonymization

Privacy Models, Data Utility, and Microaggregation-based
Inter-model Connections

Synthesis Lectures on Information Security, Privacy, & Trust

Editor
Elisa Bertino, *Purdue University*
Ravi Sandhu, *University of Texas at San Antonio*

The Synthesis Lectures Series on Information Security, Privacy, and Trust publishes 50- to 100-page publications on topics pertaining to all aspects of the theory and practice of Information Security, Privacy, and Trust. The scope largely follows the purview of premier computer security research journals such as ACM Transactions on Information and System Security, IEEE Transactions on Dependable and Secure Computing and Journal of Cryptology, and premier research conferences, such as ACM CCS, ACM SACMAT, ACM AsiaCCS, ACM CODASPY, IEEE Security and Privacy, IEEE Computer Security Foundations, ACSAC, ESORICS, Crypto, EuroCrypt and AsiaCrypt. In addition to the research topics typically covered in such journals and conferences, the series also solicits lectures on legal, policy, social, business, and economic issues addressed to a technical audience of scientists and engineers. Lectures on significant industry developments by leading practitioners are also solicited.

Database Anonymization: Privacy Models, Data Utility, and Microaggregation-based Inter-model Connections
Josep Domingo-Ferrer, David Sánchez, and Jordi Soria-Comas
2016

Automated Software Diversity
Per Larsen, Stefan Brunthaler, Lucas Davi, Ahmad-Reza Sadeghi, and Michael Franz
2015

Trust in Social Media
Jiliang Tang and Huan Liu
2015

Physically Unclonable Functions (PUFs): Applications, Models, and Future Directions
Christian Wachsmann and Ahmad-Reza Sadeghi
2014

Usable Security: History, Themes, and Challenges
Simson Garfinkel and Heather Richter Lipford
2014

Reversible Digital Watermarking: Theory and Practices
Ruchira Naskar and Rajat Subhra Chakraborty
2014

Mobile Platform Security
N. Asokan, Lucas Davi, Alexandra Dmitrienko, Stephan Heuser, Kari Kostiainen, Elena
Reshetova, and Ahmad-Reza Sadeghi
2013

Security and Trust in Online Social Networks
Barbara Carminati, Elena Ferrari, and Marco Viviani
2013

RFID Security and Privacy
Yingjiu Li, Robert H. Deng, and Elisa Bertino
2013

Hardware Malware
Christian Krieg, Adrian Dabrowski, Heidelinde Hobel, Katharina Krombholz, and Edgar Weippl
2013

Private Information Retrieval
Xun Yi, Russell Paulet, and Elisa Bertino
2013

Privacy for Location-based Services
Gabriel Ghinita
2013

Enhancing Information Security and Privacy by Combining Biometrics with
Cryptography
Sanjay G. Kanade, Dijana Petrovska-Delacrétaz, and Bernadette Dorizzi
2012

Analysis Techniques for Information Security
Anupam Datta, Somesh Jha, Ninghui Li, David Melski, and Thomas Reps
2010

Operating System Security
Trent Jaeger
2008

Database Anonymization:
Privacy Models, Data Utility, and Microaggregation-based Inter-model Connections
Josep Domingo-Ferrer, David Sánchez, and Jordi Soria-Comas

ISBN: 978-3-031-01219-8   paperback
ISBN: 978-3-031-02347-7   ebook

DOI 10.1007/978-3-031-02347-7

A Publication in the Springer series
SYNTHESIS LECTURES ON INFORMATION SECURITY, PRIVACY, & TRUST

Lecture #15
Series Editors: Elisa Bertino, *Purdue University*
                        Ravi Sandhu, *University of Texas at San Antonio*
Series ISSN
Print 1945-9742   Electronic 1945-9750

Database Anonymization

Privacy Models, Data Utility, and Microaggregation-based

Inter-model Connections

Josep Domingo-Ferrer, David Sánchez, and Jordi Soria-Comas
Universitat Rovira i Virgili, Tarragona, Catalonia

SYNTHESIS LECTURES ON INFORMATION SECURITY, PRIVACY, &
TRUST #15

ABSTRACT

The current social and economic context increasingly demands open data to improve scientific research and decision making. However, when published data refer to individual respondents, disclosure risk limitation techniques must be implemented to anonymize the data and guarantee by design the fundamental right to privacy of the subjects the data refer to. Disclosure risk limitation has a long record in the statistical and computer science research communities, who have developed a variety of privacy-preserving solutions for data releases. This Synthesis Lecture provides a comprehensive overview of the fundamentals of privacy in data releases focusing on the computer science perspective. Specifically, we detail the privacy models, anonymization methods, and utility and risk metrics that have been proposed so far in the literature. Besides, as a more advanced topic, we identify and discuss in detail connections between several privacy models (i.e., how to accumulate the privacy guarantees they offer to achieve more robust protection and when such guarantees are equivalent or complementary); we also explore the links between anonymization methods and privacy models (how anonymization methods can be used to enforce privacy models and thereby offer *ex ante* privacy guarantees). These latter topics are relevant to researchers and advanced practitioners, who will gain a deeper understanding on the available data anonymization solutions and the privacy guarantees they can offer.

KEYWORDS

data releases, privacy protection, anonymization, privacy models, statistical disclosure limitation, statistical disclosure control, microaggregation

*A tots aquells que estimem, tant si són amb nosaltres
com si perviuen en el nostre record.*

To all our loved ones, whether they are with us or stay alive in our memories.

Contents

Preface

If jet airplanes ushered in the first dramatic reduction of our world's perceived size, the next shrinking came in the mid 1990s, when the Internet became widespread and the Information Age started to become a reality. We now live in a global village and some (often quite powerful) voices proclaim that maintaining one's privacy is as hopeless as it used to be in conventional small villages. Should this be true, the ingenuity of humans would have created their own nightmare.

Whereas security is essential for organizations to survive, individuals and sometimes even companies need also some privacy to develop comfortably and lead a free life. This is the reason individual privacy is mentioned in the Universal Declaration of Human Rights (1948) and data privacy is protected by law in most Western countries. Indeed, without privacy, other fundamental rights, like freedom of speech and democracy, are impaired. The outstanding challenge is to create technology that implements those legal guarantees in a way compatible with functionality and security.

This book is devoted to privacy preservation in data releases. Indeed, in our era of big data, harnessing the enormous wealth of information available is essential to increasing the progress and well-being of humankind. The challenge is how to release data that are useful for administrations and companies to make accurate decisions without disclosing sensitive information on specific identifiable individuals.

This conflict between utility and privacy has motivated research by several communities since the 1970s, both in official statistics and computer science. Specifically, computer scientists contributed the important notion of the privacy model in the late 1990s, with k-anonymity being the first practical privacy model. The idea of a privacy model is to state *ex ante* privacy guarantees that can be attained for a particular data set using one (or several) anonymization methods.

In addition to k-anonymity, we survey here its extensions l-diversity and t-closeness, as well as the alternative paradigm of differential privacy. Further, we draw on our recent research to report connections and synergies between all these privacy models: in fact, the k-anonymity-like models and differential privacy turn out to be more related than previously thought. We also show how microaggregation, a well-known family of anonymization methods that we have developed to a large extent since the late 1990s, can be used to create anonymization methods that satisfy most of the surveyed privacy models while improving the utility of the resulting protected data.

We sincerely hope that the reader, whether academic or practitioner, will benefit from this piece of work. On our side, we have enjoyed writing it and also conducting the original research described in some of the chapters.

Josep Domingo-Ferrer, David Sánchez, and Jordi Soria-Comas
January 2016

Acknowledgments

We thank Professor Elisa Bertino for encouraging us to write this Synthesis Lecture. This work was partly supported by the European Commission (through project H2020 "CLARUS"), by the Spanish Government (through projects "ICWT" TIN2012-32757 and "SmartGlacis" TIN2014-57364-C2-1-R), by the Government of Catalonia (under grant 2014 SGR 537), and by the Templeton World Charity Foundation (under project "CO-UTILITY"). Josep Domingo-Ferrer is partially supported as an ICREA-Acadèmia researcher by the Government of Catalonia. The authors are with the UNESCO Chair in Data Privacy, but the opinions expressed in this work are the authors' own and do not necessarily reflect the views of UNESCO or any of the funders.

Josep Domingo-Ferrer, David Sánchez, and Jordi Soria-Comas
January 2016

CHAPTER 1

Introduction

The current social and economic context increasingly demands open data to improve planning, scientific research, market analysis, etc. In particular, the public sector is pushed to release as much information as possible for the sake of transparency. Organizations releasing data include national statistical institutes (whose core mission is to publish statistical information), healthcare authorities (which occasionally release epidemiologic information) or even private organizations (which sometimes publish consumer surveys). When published data refer to individual respondents, care must be exerted for the privacy of the latter not to be violated. It should be *de facto* impossible to relate the published data to specific individuals. Indeed, supplying data to national statistical institutes is compulsory in most countries but, in return, these institutes commit to preserving the privacy of the respondents. Hence, rather than publishing accurate information for each individual, the aim should be to provide useful statistical information, that is, to preserve as much as possible in the released data the statistical properties of the original data.

Disclosure risk limitation has a long tradition in official statistics, where privacy-preserving databases on individuals are called *statistical databases*. Inference control in statistical databases, also known as *Statistical Disclosure Control (SDC)*, *Statistical Disclosure Limitation (SDL)*, *database anonymization*, or *database sanitization*, is a discipline that seeks to protect data so that they can be published without revealing confidential information that can be linked to specific individuals among those to whom the data correspond.

Disclosure limitation has also been a topic of interest in the computer science research community, which refers to it as *Privacy Preserving Data Publishing (PPDP)* and *Privacy Preserving Data Mining (PPDM)*. The latter focuses on protecting the privacy of the results of data mining tasks, whereas the former focuses on the publication of data of individuals.

Whereas both SDC and PPDP pursue the same objective, SDC proposes protection mechanisms that are more concerned with the utility of the data and offer only vague (i.e., *ex post*) privacy guarantees, whereas PPDP seeks to attain an *ex ante* privacy guarantee (by adhering to a privacy model), but offers no utility guarantees.

In this book we provide an exhaustive overview of the fundamentals of privacy in data releases, including privacy models, anonymization/SDC methods, and utility and risk metrics that have been proposed so far in the literature. Moreover, as a more advanced topic, we discuss in detail the connections between several proposed privacy models (how to accumulate the guarantees offered by different privacy models to achieve more robust protection and when are such guarantees equivalent or complementary). We also propose bridges between SDC methods and privacy models (i.e., how specific SDC methods can be used to satisfy specific privacy models and thereby offer *ex ante* privacy guarantees).

The book is organized as follows.

- Chapter 2 details the basic notions of privacy in data releases: types of data releases, privacy threats and metrics, and families of SDC methods.

- Chapter 3 offers a comprehensive overview of SDC methods, classified into perturbative and non-perturbative ones.

- Chapter 4 describes how disclosure risk can be empirically quantified via record linkage.

- Chapter 5 discusses the well-known k-anonymity privacy model, which is focused on preventing re-identification of individuals, and details which data protection mechanisms can be used to enforce it.

- Chapter 6 describes two extensions of k-anonymity (l-diversity and t-closeness) focused on offering protection against attribute disclosure.

- Chapter 7 presents in detail how t-closeness can be attained on top of k-anonymity by relying on data microaggregation (i.e., a specific SDC method based on data clustering).

- Chapter 8 describes the differential privacy model, which mainly focuses on providing sanitized answers with robust privacy guarantees to specific queries. We also explain SDC techniques that can be used to attain differential privacy. We also discuss in detail the relationship between differential privacy and k-anonymity-based models (t-closeness, specifically).

- Chapters 9 and 10 present two state-of-the-art approaches to offer utility-preserving differentially private data releases by relying on the notion of k-anonymous data releases and on multivariate and univariate microaggregation, respectively.

- Chapter 11 summarizes general conclusions and introduces some topics for future research. More specific conclusions are given at the end of each chapter.

CHAPTER 2

Privacy in Data Releases

References to privacy were already present in the writings of Greek philosophers when they distinguish the *outer* (public) from the *inner* (private). Nowadays privacy is considered a fundamental right of individuals [34, 101]. Despite this long history, the formal description of the "right to privacy" is quite recent. It was coined by Warren and Brandeis, back in 1890, in an article [103] published in the *Harvard Law Review*. These authors presented laws as dynamic systems for the protection of individuals whose evolution is triggered by social, political, and economic changes. In particular, the conception of the right to privacy is triggered by the technical advances and new business models of the time. Quoting Warren and Brandeis:

> Instantaneous photographs and newspaper enterprise have invaded the sacred precincts of private and domestic life; and numerous mechanical devices threaten to make good the prediction that what is whispered in the closet shall be proclaimed from the house-tops.

Warren and Brandeis argue that the "right to privacy" was already existent in many areas of the common law; they only gathered all these sparse legal concepts, and put them into focus under their common denominator. Within the legal framework of the time, the "right to privacy" was part of the right to life, one of the three fundamental individual rights recognized by the U.S. constitution.

Privacy concerns revived again with the invention of computers [31] and information exchange networks, which skyrocketed information collection, storage and processing capabilities. The generalization of population surveys was a consequence. The focus was then on data protection.

Nowadays, privacy is widely considered a fundamental right, and it is supported by international treaties and many constitutional laws. For example, the Universal Declaration of Human Rights (1948) devotes its Article 12 to privacy. In fact, privacy has gained worldwide recognition and it applies to a wide range of situations such as: avoiding external meddling at home, limiting the use of surveillance technologies, controlling processing and dissemination of personal data, etc.

As far as the protection of individuals' data is concerned, privacy legislation is based on several principles [69, 101]: collection limitation, purpose specification, use limitation, data quality, security safeguards, openness, individual participation, and accountability. Although, with the appearance of big data, it is unclear if any of these principles is really effective [93].

Among all the aspects that relate to data privacy, we are especially interested in data dissemination. Dissemination is, for instance, the primary task of National Statistical Institutes. These aim at offering an accurate picture of society; to that end, they collect and publish statistical data on a wide range of aspects such as economy, population, etc. Legislation usually assimilates privacy violations in data dissemination to individual identifiability [1, 2]; for instance, Title 13, Chapter 1.1 of the U.S. Code states that "no individual should be re-identifiable in the released data."

For a more comprehensive review of the history of privacy, check [43]. A more visual perspective of privacy is given by the timelines [3, 4]. In [3] key privacy-related events between 1600 (when it was a civic duty to keep an eye on your neighbors) and 2008 (after the U.S. Patriot Act and the inception of Facebook) are listed. In [4] key moments that have shaped privacy-related laws are depicted.

2.1   TYPES OF DATA RELEASES

The type of data being released determines the potential threats to privacy as well as the most suitable protection methods. Statistical databases come in three main formats.

- *Microdata*. The term "microdata" refers to a record that contains information related to a specific individual (a citizen or a company). A microdata release aims at publishing raw data, that is, a set of microdata records.

- *Tabular data*. Cross-tabulated values showing aggregate values for groups of individuals are released. The term contingency (or frequency) table is used when counts are released, and the term "magnitude table" is used for other aggregate magnitudes. These types of data is the classical output of official statistics.

- *Queryable databases*, that is, interactive databases to which the user can submit statistical queries (sums, averages, etc.).

Our focus in subsequent chapters is on microdata releases. Microdata offer the greatest level of flexibility among all types of data releases: data users are not confined to a specific prefixed view of data; they are able to carry out any kind of custom analysis on the released data. However, microdata releases are also the most challenging for the privacy of individuals.

2.2   MICRODATA SETS

A microdata set can be represented as a table (matrix) where each row refers to a different individual and each column contains information regarding one of the attributes collected. We use X to denote the collected microdata file. We assume that X contains information about n respondents and m attributes. We use x_i to refer to the record contributed by respondent i, and x^j (or X^j) to refer to attribute j. The value of attribute j for respondent i is denoted by x_i^j.

The attributes in a microdata set are usually classified in the following non-exclusive categories.

- *Identifiers.* An attribute is an identifier if it provides unambiguous re-identification of the individual to which the record refers. Some examples of identifier attributes are the social security number, the passport number, etc. If a record contains an identifier, any sensitive information contained in other attributes may immediately be linked to a specific individual. To avoid direct re-identification of an individual, identifier attributes must be removed or encrypted. In the following chapters, we assume that identifier attributes have previously been removed.

- *Quasi-identifiers.* Unlike an identifier, a quasi-identifier attribute alone does not lead to record re-identification. However, in combination with other quasi-identifier attributes, it may allow unambiguous re-identification of some individuals. For example, [99] shows that 87% of the population in the U.S. can be unambiguously identified by combining a 5-digit ZIP code, birth date, and sex. Removing quasi-identifier attributes, as proposed for the identifiers, is not possible, because quasi-identifiers are most of the time required to perform any useful analysis of the data. Deciding whether a specific attribute should be considered a quasi-identifier is a thorny issue. In practice, any information an intruder has about an individual can be used in record re-identification. For uninformed intruders, only the attributes available in an external non-anonymized data set should be classified as quasi-identifiers; in the presence of informed intruders any attribute may potentially be a quasi-identifier. Thus, in the strictest case, to make sure all potential quasi-identifiers have been removed, one ought to remove all attributes (!).

- *Confidential attributes.* Confidential attributes hold sensitive information on the individuals that took part in the data collection process (e.g., salary, health condition, sex orientation, etc.). The primary goal of microdata protection techniques is to prevent intruders from learning confidential information about a specific individual. This goal involves not only preventing the intruder from determining the exact value that a confidential attribute takes for some individual, but also preventing accurate inferences on the value of that attribute (such as bounding it).

- *Non-confidential attributes.* Non-confidential attributes are those that do not belong to any of the previous categories. As they do not contain sensitive information about individuals and cannot be used for record re-identification, they do not affect our discussion on disclosure limitation for microdata sets. Therefore, we assume that none of the attributes in X belong to this category.

2.3   FORMALIZING PRIVACY

A first attempt to come up with a formal definition of privacy was made by Dalenius in [14]. He stated that access to the released data should not allow any attacker to increase his knowledge about confidential information related to a specific individual. In other words, the prior and the posterior beliefs about an individual in the database should be similar. Because the ultimate goal in privacy is to keep the secrecy of sensitive information about specific individuals, this is a natural definition of privacy. However, Dalenius' definition is too strict to be useful in practice. This was illustrated with two examples [29]. The first one considers an adversary whose prior view is that everyone has two left feet. By accessing a statistical database, the adversary learns that almost everybody has one left foot and one right foot, thus modifying his posterior belief about individuals to a great extent. In the second example, the use of auxiliary information makes things worse. Suppose that a statistical database teaches the average height of a group of individuals, and that it is not possible to learn this information in any other way. Suppose also that the actual height of a person is considered to be a sensitive piece of information. Let the attacker have the following side information: "Adam is one centimeter taller than the average English man." Access to the database teaches Adam's height, while having the side information but no database access teaches much less. Thus, Dalenius' view of privacy is not feasible in presence of background information (if any utility is to be provided).

The privacy criteria used in practice offer only limited disclosure control guarantees. Two main views of privacy are used for microdata releases: anonymity (it should not be possible to re-identify any individual in the published data) and confidentiality or secrecy (access to the released data should not reveal confidential information related to any specific individual).

The confidentiality view of privacy is closer to Dalenius' proposal, being the main difference that it limits the amount of information provided by the data set rather than the change between prior and posterior beliefs about an individual. There are several approaches to attain confidentiality. A basic example of SDC technique that gives confidentiality is noise addition. By adding a random noise to a confidential data item, we mask its value: we report a value drawn from a random distribution rather than the actual value. The amount of noise added determines the level of confidentiality.

The anonymity view of privacy seeks to hide each individual in a group. This is indeed quite intuitive a view of privacy: the privacy of an individual is protected if we are not able to distinguish her from other individuals in a group. This view of privacy is commonly used in legal frameworks. For instance, the U.S. *Health Insurance Portability and Accountability Act (HIPAA)* of 1996 requires removing several attributes that could potentially identify an individual; in this way, the individual stays anonymous. However, we should keep in mind that if the value of the confidential attribute has a small variability within the group of indistinguishable individuals, disclosure still happens for these individuals: even if we are not able to tell which record belongs to each of the individuals, the low variability of the confidential attribute gives us a good estimation of its actual value.

The Health Insurance Portability and Accountability Act (HIPAA)

The Privacy Rule allows a covered entity to de-identify data by removing all 18 elements that could be used to identify the individual or the individual's relatives, employers, or household members; these elements are enumerated in the Privacy Rule. The covered entity also must have no actual knowledge that the remaining information could be used alone or in combination with other information to identify the individual who is the subject of the information. Under this method, the identifiers that must be removed are the following:

- Names.

- All geographic subdivisions smaller than a state, including street address, city, county, precinct, ZIP code, and their equivalent geographical codes, except for the initial three digits of a ZIP code if, according to the current publicly available data from the Bureau of the Census:

    - The geographic unit formed by combining all ZIP codes with the same three initial digits contains more than 20,000 people.

    - The initial three digits of a ZIP code for all such geographic units containing 20,000 or fewer people are changed to 000.

- All elements of dates (except year) for dates directly related to an individual, including birth date, admission date, discharge date, date of death; and all ages over 89 and all elements of dates (including year) indicative of such age, except that such ages and elements may be aggregated into a single category of age 90 or older.

- Telephone numbers.

- Facsimile numbers.

- Electronic mail addresses.

- Social security numbers.

- Medical record numbers.

- Health plan beneficiary numbers.

- Account numbers.

- Certificate/license numbers.

- Vehicle identifiers and serial numbers, including license plate numbers.

- Device identifiers and serial numbers.

- Web universal resource locators (URLs).

- Internet protocol (IP) address numbers.

- Biometric identifiers, including fingerprints and voiceprints.

- Full-face photographic images and any comparable images.

- Any other unique identifying number, characteristic, or code, unless otherwise permitted by the Privacy Rule for re-identification.

2.4 DISCLOSURE RISK IN MICRODATA SETS

When publishing a microdata file, the data collector must guarantee that no sensitive information about specific individuals is disclosed. Usually two types of disclosure are considered in microdata sets [44].

- *Identity disclosure.* This type of disclosure violates privacy viewed as anonymity. It occurs when the intruder is able to associate a record in the released data set with the individual that originated it. After re-identification, the intruder associates the values of the confidential attributes for the record to the re-identified individual. Two main approaches are usually employed to measure identity disclosure risk: uniqueness and reidentification.

    - *Uniqueness.* Roughly speaking, the risk of identity disclosure is measured as the probability that rare combinations of attribute values in the released protected data are indeed rare in the original population the data come from.

    - *Record linkage.* This is an empirical approach to evaluate the risk of disclosure. In this case, the data protector (also known as data controller) uses a record linkage algorithm (or several such algorithms) to link each record in the anonymized data with a record in the original data set. Since the protector knows the real correspondence between original and anonymized records, he can determine the percentage of correctly linked pairs, which he uses to estimate the number of re-identifications that might be obtained by a specialized intruder. If this number is unacceptably high, then more intense anonymization by the controller is needed before the anonymized data set is ready for release.

- *Attribute disclosure.* This type of disclosure violates privacy viewed as confidentiality. It occurs when access to the released data allows the intruder to determine the value of a confidential attribute of an individual with enough accuracy.

The above two types of disclosure are independent. Even if identity disclosure happens, there may not be attribute disclosure if the confidential attributes in the released data set have been masked. On the other side, attribute disclosure may still happen even without identity disclosure. For example, imagine that the salary is one of the confidential attributes and the job is a quasi-identifier attribute; if an intruder is interested in a specific individual whose job he knows to be "accountant" and there are several accountants in the data set (including the target individual), the intruder will be unable to re-identify the individual's record based only on her job, but he will be able to lower-bound and upper-bound the individual's salary (which lies between the minimum and the maximum salary of all the accountants in the data set). Specifically, attribute disclosure happens if the range of possible salary values for the matching records is narrow.

2.5   MICRODATA ANONYMIZATION

To avoid disclosure, data collectors do not publish the original microdata set X, but a modified version Y of it. This data set Y is called the protected, anonymized, or sanitized version of X. Microdata protection methods can generate the protected data set by either masking the original data or generating synthetic data.

- *Masking.* The protected data Y are generated by modifying the original records in X. Masking induces a relation between the records in Y and the original records in X. When applied to quasi-identifier attributes, the identity behind each record is masked (which yields anonymity). When applied to confidential attributes, the values of the confidential data are masked (which yields confidentiality, even if the subject to whom the record corresponds might still be re-identifiable). Masking methods can in turn be divided in two categories depending on their effect on the original data.

    - *Perturbative masking.* The microdata set is distorted before publication. The perturbation method used should be such that the statistics computed on the perturbed data set do not differ significantly from the statistics that would be obtained on the original data set. Noise addition, microaggregation, data/rank swapping, microdata rounding, resampling, and PRAM are examples of perturbative masking methods.

    - *Non-perturbative masking.* Non-perturbative methods do not alter data; rather, they produce partial suppressions or reductions of detail/coarsening in the original data set. Sampling, global recoding, top and bottom coding, and local suppression are examples of non-perturbative masking methods.

- *Synthetic data.* The protected data set Y consists of randomly simulated records that do not directly derive from the records in X; the only connection between X and Y is that the latter preserves some statistics from the former (typically a model relating the attributes in X). The generation of a synthetic data set takes three steps [27, 77]: (i) a model for the population is proposed, (ii) the model is adjusted to the original data set X, and (iii) the synthetic data set Y is generated by drawing from the model. There are three types of synthetic data sets:

- *Fully synthetic* [77], where every attribute value for every record has been synthesized. The population units (subjects) contained in Y are not the original population units in X but a new sample from the underlying population.

- *Partially synthetic* [74], where only the data items (the attribute values) with high risk of disclosure are synthesized. The population units in Y are the same population units in X (in particular, X and Y have the same number of records).

- *Hybrid* [19, 65], where the original data set is mixed with a fully synthetic data set.

In a fully synthetic data set any dependency between X and Y must come from the model. In other words, X and Y are independent conditionally to the adjusted model. The disclosure risk in fully synthetic data sets is usually low, as we justify next. On the one side, the population units in Y are not the original population units in X. On the other side, the information about the original data X conveyed by Y is only the one incorporated by the model, which is usually limited to some statistical properties. In a partially synthetic data set, the disclosure risk is reduced by replacing the values in the original data set at a higher risk of disclosure with simulated values. The simulated values assigned to an individual should be representative but are not directly related to her. In hybrid data sets, the level of protection we get is the lowest; mixing original and synthetic records breaks the conditional independence between the original data and the synthetic data. The parameters of the mixture determine the amount of dependence.

2.6   MEASURING INFORMATION LOSS

The evaluation of the utility of the protected data set must be based on the intended uses of the data. The closer the results obtained for these uses between the original and the protected data, the more utility is preserved. However, very often, microdata protection cannot be performed in a data use specific manner, due to the following reasons.

- Potential data uses are very diverse and it may even be hard to identify them all at the moment of the data release.

- Even if all the data uses could be identified, releasing several versions of the same original data set so that the i-th version has been optimized for the i-th data use may result in unexpected disclosure.

Since data must often be protected with no specific use in mind, it is usually more appropriate to refer to information loss rather than to utility. Measures of information loss provide generic ways for the data protector to assess how much harm is being inflicted to the data by a particular data masking technique.

Information loss measures for numerical data. Assume a microdata set X with n individuals (records) $x_1, \ldots, x_n$ and m continuous attributes $x^1, \ldots, x^m$. Let Y be the protected microdata set. The following tools are useful to characterize the information contained in the data set:

- Covariance matrices V (on X) and V' (on Y).

- Correlation matrices R and R'.

- Correlation matrices RF and RF' between the m attributes and the m factors $PC_1, PC_2, \ldots, PC_p$ obtained through principal components analysis.

- Communality between each of the m attributes and the first principal component PC_1 (or other principal components PC_i's). Communality is the percent of each attribute that is explained by PC_1 (or PC_i). Let C be the vector of communalities for X, and C' the corresponding vector for Y.

- Factor score coefficient matrices F and F'. Matrix F contains the factors that should multiply each attribute in X to obtain its projection on each principal component. F' is the corresponding matrix for Y.

There does not seem to be a single quantitative measure which completely reflects the structural differences between X and Y. Therefore, in [25, 87] it was proposed to measure the information loss through the discrepancies between matrices X, V, R, RF, C, and F obtained on the original data and the corresponding X', V', R', RF', C', and F' obtained on the protected data set. In particular, discrepancy between correlations is related to the information loss for data uses such as regressions and cross-tabulations. Matrix discrepancy can be measured in at least three ways.

- *Mean square error.* Sum of squared componentwise differences between pairs of matrices, divided by the number of cells in either matrix.

- *Mean absolute error.* Sum of absolute componentwise differences between pairs of matrices, divided by the number of cells in either matrix.

- *Mean variation.* Sum of absolute percent variation of components in the matrix computed on the protected data with respect to components in the matrix computed on the original data, divided by the number of cells in either matrix. This approach has the advantage of not being affected by scale changes of attributes.

Information loss measures for categorical data. These have been usually based on direct comparison of categorical values, comparison of contingency tables, or on Shannon's entropy [25]. More recently, the importance of the semantics underlying categorical data for data utility has been realized [60, 83]. As a result, semantically grounded information loss measures that exploits the formal semantics provided by structured knowledge sources (such as taxonomies or ontologies) have been proposed both to measure the practical utility and to guide the sanitization algorithms in terms of the preservation of data semantics [23, 57, 59].

Bounded information loss measures. The information loss measures discussed above are unbounded, i.e., they do not take values in a predefined interval. On the other hand, as discussed below, disclosure risk measures are naturally bounded (the risk of disclosure is naturally bounded between 0 and 1). Defining bounded information loss measures may be convenient to enable the data protector to trade off information loss against disclosure risk. In [61], probabilistic information loss measures bounded between 0 and 1 are proposed for continuous data.

Propensity scores: a global information loss measure for all types of data. In [105], an information loss measure U applicable to continuous and categorical microdata was proposed. It is computed as follows.

1. Merge the original microdata set X and the anonymized microdata set Y, and add to the merged data set a binary attribute T with value 1 for the anonymized records and 0 for the original records.

2. Regress T on the rest of attributes of the merged data set and call the adjusted attribute $\hat{T}$. For categorical attributes, logistic regression can be used.

3. Let the *propensity score* $\hat{p}_i$ of record i of the merged data set be the value of $\hat{T}$ for record i. Then the utility of Y is high if the propensity scores of the anonymized and original records are similar (this means that, based on the regression model used, anonymized records cannot be distinguished from original records).

4. Hence, if the number of original and anonymized records is the same, say N, a utility measure is

$$U = \frac{1}{N} \sum_{i=1}^{N} [\hat{p}_i - 1/2]^2.$$

The farther U from 0, the more information loss, and conversely.

2.7 TRADING OFF INFORMATION LOSS AND DISCLOSURE RISK

The goal of SDC to modify data so that sufficient protection is provided at minimum information loss suggests that a good anonymization method is one close to optimizing the trade-off between disclosure risk and information loss. Several approaches have been proposed to handle this trade-off. Here we discuss SDC scores and R-U maps.

SDC scores

An SDC score is a formula that combines the effects of information loss and disclosure risk in a single figure. Having adopted an SDC score as a good trade-off measure, the goal is to optimize the score value. Following this idea, [25] proposed a score for method performance rating based on the average of information loss and disclosure risk measures. For each method M and parameterization P, the following score is computed:

$$Score_{M,P}(X,Y) = \frac{IL(X,Y) + DR(X,Y)}{2}$$

where *IL* is an information loss measure, *DR* is a disclosure risk measure, and *Y* is the protected data set obtained after applying method *M* with parameterization *P* to an original data set *X*. In [25] *IL* and *DR* were computed using a weighted combination of several information loss and disclosure risk measures. With the resulting score, a ranking of masking methods (and their parametrizations) was obtained. Using a score permits regarding the selection of a masking method and its parameters as an optimization problem: a masking method can be applied to the original data file and then a post-masking optimization procedure can be applied to decrease the score obtained (that is, to reduce information loss and disclosure risk). On the negative side, no specific score weighting can do justice to all methods. Thus, when ranking methods, the values of all measures of information loss and disclosure risk should be supplied along with the overall score.

R-U maps

A tool which may be enlightening when trying to construct a score or, more generally, optimize the trade-off between information loss and disclosure risk is a graphical representation of pairs of measures (disclosure risk, information loss) or their equivalents (disclosure risk, data utility). Such maps are called R-U confidentiality maps [28]. Here, R stands for disclosure risk and U for data utility. In its most basic form, an R-U confidentiality map is the set of paired values (R,U) of disclosure risk and data utility that correspond to the various strategies for data release (e.g., variations on a parameter). Such (R,U) pairs are typically plotted in a two-dimensional graph, so that the user can easily grasp the influence of a particular method and/or parameter choice.

2.8   SUMMARY

This chapter has presented a broad overview of disclosure risk limitation. We have identified the privacy threats (identity and/or attribute disclosure), and we have introduced the main families of SDC methods (data masking via perturbative and non-perturbative methods, as well as synthetic data generation). Also, we have surveyed disclosure risk and information loss metrics and we have discussed how risk and information loss can be traded off in view of finding the best SDC method and parameterization.

CHAPTER 3

Anonymization Methods for Microdata

It was commented in Section 2.5 that the protected data set Y was generated either by masking the original data set X or by building it from scratch based on a model of the original data. Microdata masking techniques were further classified into perturbative masking (which distorts the original data and leads to the publication of non-truthful data) and non-perturbative masking (which reduces the amount of information, either by suppressing some of the data or by reducing the level of detail, but preserves truthfulness). This chapter classifies and reviews some well-known SDC techniques. These techniques are not only useful on their own but they also constitute the basis to enforce the privacy guarantees required by privacy models.

3.1   NON-PERTURBATIVE MASKING METHODS

Non-perturbative methods do not alter data; rather, they produce partial suppressions or reductions of detail in the original data set.

Sampling

Instead of publishing the original microdata file X, what is published is a sample S of the original set of records [104]. Sampling methods are suitable for categorical microdata [58], but for continuous microdata they should probably be combined with other masking methods. The reason is that sampling alone leaves a continuous attribute unperturbed for all records in S. Thus, if any continuous attribute is present in an external administrative public file, unique matches with the published sample are very likely: indeed, given a continuous attribute and two respondents x_i and x_j, it is unlikely that both respondents will take the same value for the continuous attribute unless $x_i = x_j$ (this is true even if the continuous attribute has been truncated to represent it digitally). If, for a continuous identifying attribute, the score of a respondent is only approximately known by an attacker, it might still make sense to use sampling methods to protect that attribute. However, assumptions on restricted attacker resources are perilous and may prove definitely too optimistic if good quality external administrative files are at hand.

Generalization

This technique is also known as global recoding in the statistical disclosure control literature. For a categorical attribute X^i, several categories are combined to form new (less specific) categories, thus resulting in a new Y^i with $|Dom(Y^i)| < |Dom(X^i)|$ where $|\cdot|$ is the cardinality operator and $Dom(\cdot)$ is the domain where the attribute takes values. For a continuous attribute, generalization means replacing X^i by another attribute Y^i which is a discretized version of X^i. In other words, a potentially infinite range $Dom(X^i)$ is mapped onto a finite range $Dom(Y^i)$. This is the technique used in the μ-Argus SDC package [45]. This technique is more appropriate for categorical microdata, where it helps disguise records with strange combinations of categorical attributes. Generalization is used heavily by statistical offices.

Example 3.1   If there is a record with "Marital status = Widow/er" and "Age = 17," generalization could be applied to "Marital status" to create a broader category "Widow/er or divorced," so that the probability of the above record being unique would diminish. Generalization can also be used on a continuous attribute, but the inherent discretization leads very often to an unaffordable loss of information. Also, arithmetical operations that were straightforward on the original X^i are no longer easy or intuitive on the discretized Y^i.

Top and bottom coding

Top and bottom coding are special cases of generalization which can be used on attributes that can be ranked, that is, continuous or categorical ordinal. The idea is that top values (those above a certain threshold) are lumped together to form a new category. The same is done for bottom values (those below a certain threshold).

Local suppression

This is a masking method in which certain values of individual attributes are suppressed with the aim of increasing the set of records agreeing on a combination of key values. Ways to combine local suppression and generalization are implemented in the μ-Argus SDC package [45].

   If a continuous attribute X^i is part of a set of key attributes, then each combination of key values is probably unique. Since it does not make sense to systematically suppress the values of X^i, we conclude that local suppression is rather oriented to categorical attributes.

3.2   PERTURBATIVE MASKING METHODS

Noise addition

Additive noise is a family of perturbative masking methods. The values in the original data set are masked by adding some random noise. The statistical properties of the noise being added determine the effect of noise addition on the original data set. Several noise addition procedures have been developed, each of them with the aim to better preserve the statistical properties of the original data.

- *Masking by uncorrelated noise addition.* The vector of observations, x^i, for the i-th attribute of the original data set X^i is replaced by a vector $y^i = x^i + e^i$ where e^i is a vector of normally distributed errors. Let e_k^i and e_l^i be, respectively, the k-th and l-th components of vector e^i. We have that e_k^i and e_l^i are independent and drawn from a normal distribution $N(0, s_i^2)$. The usual approach is for the variance of the noise added to attribute X^i to be proportional to the variance of X^i; that is, $s_i^2 = \alpha Var(x^i)$. The term "uncorrelated" is used to mean that there is no correlation between the noise added to different attributes.

This method preserves means and covariances,

$$E(y^i) = E(x^i) + E(e^i) = E(x^i);$$

$$Cov(y^i, y^j) = Cov(x^i, x^j).$$

However, neither variances nor correlations are preserved

$$Var(y^i) = Var(x^i) + Var(e^i) = (1 + \alpha)Var(x^i);$$

$$\rho_{y^i, y^j} = \frac{Cov(y^i, y^j)}{\sqrt{Var(y^i)Var(y^j)}} = \frac{1}{1 + \alpha}\rho_{y^i, y^j}.$$

- *Masking by correlated noise addition.* Noise addition alone always modifies the variance of the original attributes. Thus, if we want to preserve the correlation coefficients of the original data, the covariances must be modified. This is what masking by correlated noise does. By taking the covariance matrix of the noise to be proportional to the covariance matrix of the original data we have:

$$E(y^i) = E(x^i) + E(e^i) = E(x^i);$$

$$Cov(y^i, y^j) = Cov(x^i, x^j) + Cov(e^i, e^j) = (1 + \alpha)Cov(x^i, x^j);$$

$$Var(y^i) = Var(x^i) + Var(e^i) = (1 + \alpha)Var(x^i);$$

$$\rho_{y^i, y^j} = \frac{Cov(y^i, y^j)}{\sqrt{Var(y^i)Var(y^j)}} = \frac{1 + \alpha}{1 + \alpha}\rho_{y^i, y^j} = \rho_{y^i, y^j}.$$

- *Masking by noise addition and linear transformation.* In [48], a method is proposed that ensures by additional transformations that the sample covariance matrix of the masked attributes is an unbiased estimator for the covariance matrix of the original attributes.

- *Masking by noise addition and nonlinear transformation.* Combining simple additive noise and nonlinear transformation has also been proposed, in such a way that application to discrete attributes is possible and univariate distributions are preserved. Unfortunately, the application of this method is very time-consuming and requires expert knowledge on the data set and the algorithm. See [44] for more details.

Noise addition methods with normal distributions are naturally meant for continuous data, even though some adaptations to categorical data have been also proposed [76]. Moreover, the introduction of the differential privacy model for disclosure control has motivated the use of other noise distributions. The focus here is on the preservation of the privacy guarantees of the model rather than the statistical properties of the data. The addition of uncorrelated Laplace distributed noise is the most common approach to attain differential privacy [29]. For the case of discrete data, the geometric distribution [33] is a better alternative to the Laplace distributed noise. It has also been shown that the Laplace distribution is not the optimal noise in attaining differential privacy for continuous data [92].

Data/rank swapping

Data swapping was originally presented as an SDC method for databases containing only categorical attributes. The basic idea behind the method is to transform a database by exchanging values of confidential attributes among individual records. Records are exchanged in such a way that low-order frequency counts or marginals are maintained.

In spite of the original procedure not being very used in practice, its basic idea had a clear influence in subsequent methods. A variant of data swapping for microdata is rank swapping, which will be described next in some detail. Although originally described only for ordinal attributes [36], rank swapping can also be used for any numerical attribute. See Algorithm 1. First, values of an attribute A are ranked in ascending order, then each ranked value of A is swapped with another ranked value randomly chosen within a restricted range (e.g., the rank of two swapped values cannot differ by more than p% of the total number of records, where p is an input parameter).

This algorithm is independently used on each original attribute in the original data set. It is reasonable to expect that multivariate statistics computed from data swapped with this algorithm will be less distorted than those computed after an unconstrained swap.

Microaggregation

Microaggregation is a family of SDC techniques for continuous microdata. The rationale behind microaggregation is that confidentiality rules in use allow publication of microdata sets if records correspond to groups of k or more individuals, where no individual dominates (i.e., contributes too much to) the group and k is a threshold value. Strict application of such confidentiality rules leads to replacing individual values with values computed on small aggregates (microaggregates) prior to publication. This is the basic principle of microaggregation. To obtain microaggregates in a microdata set with n records, these are combined to form g groups of size at least k. For each attribute, the average value over each group is computed and is used to replace each of the original averaged values. Groups are formed using a criterion of maximal similarity. Once the procedure has been completed, the resulting (modified) records can be published. The optimal k-partition (from the information loss point of view) is defined to be the one that maximizes within-group

---

Algorithm 1 Rank swapping with swapping restricted to p%

Data: X: original data set

   p: percentage of records within the allowed swapping range

Result The rank swapped data set

For Each attribute X^i **Do**

   Order the X by attribute X^i (records with missing values for attribute X^i as well as records with value set to top- or bottom-code are not considered).

   Let N be the number of records considered.

   Tag all considered records as unswapped.

   While there are unswapped records **Do**

      Let i be the lowest unswapped rank.

      Randomly select an unswapped record with rank in the interval $[i + 1, M]$ with $M = \min\{N, i + p * N/100\}$. Suppose the selected record has rank j.

      Swap the value of attribute A between records ranked i and j.

   End While

End For

Return X

---

homogeneity; the higher the within-group homogeneity, the lower the information loss, since microaggregation replaces values in a group by the group centroid. The sum of squares criterion is common to measure homogeneity in clustering. The within-groups sum of squares SSE is defined as:

$$SSE = \sum_{i=1}^{g} \sum_{j=1}^{n_i} (x_{ij} - \bar{x}_i)'(x_{ij} - \bar{x}_i).$$

The between-groups sum of squares SSA is

$$SSA = \sum_{i=1}^{g} n_i (\bar{x}_i - \bar{x})'(\bar{x}_i - \bar{x}).$$

The total sum of squares is $SST = SSA + SSE$ or explicitly

$$SST = \sum_{i=1}^{g} \sum_{j=1}^{n_i} (x_{ij} - \bar{x})'(x_{ij} - \bar{x}).$$

The lower the SSE, the higher the within group homogeneity. Thus, in terms of sums of squares, the optimal k-partition is the one that minimizes SSE (or equivalently, maximizes SSA).

   Given a microdata set consisting of p attributes, these can be microaggregated together or partitioned into several groups of attributes and then microaggregated. Also, the way to form groups may vary. Several taxonomies are possible to classify the microaggregation algorithms in the literature: (i) fixed group size [17, 26, 45] vs. variable group size [21, 49, 57]; (ii) exact optimal (only for the univariate case, [41]) vs. heuristic microaggregation (the rest of the microaggregation literature); (iii) categorical [26, 57] vs. continuous (the rest of the references cited in this paragraph). Also, depending on whether they deal with one or several attributes at a time, microaggregation methods can be classified into univariate and multivariate.

- Univariate methods deal with multi-attribute data sets by microaggregating one attribute at a time. Input records are sorted by the first attribute, then groups of successive k values of the first attribute are created and all values within that group are replaced by the group representative (e.g., centroid). The same procedure is repeated for the rest of the attributes. Notice that all attribute values of each record are moved together when sorting records by a particular attribute; hence, the relation between the attribute values within each record is preserved. This approach is known as *individual ranking* [16, 17]. Individual ranking just reduces the variability of attributes, thereby providing some anonymization. In [25] it was shown that individual ranking causes low information loss and, thus, its output better preserves analytical utility. However, the disclosure risk in the anonymized output remains unacceptably high [22].

- To deal with several attributes at a time, the trivial option is to map multi-attribute data sets to univariate data by projecting the former onto a single axis (e.g., using the sum of z-scores or the first principal component, see [16]) and then use univariate microaggregation on the univariate data. Another option avoiding the information loss due to single-axis projection is to use *multivariate microaggregation* able to deal with unprojected multi-attribute data [21]. If we define optimal microaggregation as finding a partition in groups of size at least k such that within-groups homogeneity is maximum, it turns out that, while optimal univariate microaggregation can be solved in polynomial time [41], unfortunately optimal multivariate microaggregation is NP-hard [70]. This justifies the use of heuristic methods for multivariate microaggregation, such as the MDAV (Maximum Distance to Average Vector, [20, 26]). In any case, multivariate microaggregation leads to higher information loss than individual ranking [25].

To illustrate these approaches, we next give the details of the MDAV heuristic algorithm for multivariate fixed group size microaggregation on unprojected continuous data.

1. Compute the average record $\bar{x}$ of all records in the data set. Consider the most distant record x_r to the average record $\bar{x}$ (using the squared Euclidean distance).

2. Find the most distant record x_s from the record x_r considered in the previous step.

3. Form two groups around x_r and x_s, respectively. One group contains x_r and the $k-1$ records closest to x_r. The other group contains x_s and the $k-1$ records closest to x_s.

4. If there are at least $3k$ records which do not belong to any of the two groups formed in Step 3, go to Step 1 taking as new data set the previous data set minus the groups formed in the last instance of Step 3.

5. If there are between $3k - 1$ and $2k$ records which do not belong to any of the two groups formed in Step 3: a) compute the average record $\bar{x}$ of the remaining records; b) find the most distant record x_r from $\bar{x}$; c) form a group containing x_r and the $k - 1$ records closest to x_r; d) form another group containing the rest of records. Exit the algorithm.

6. If there are fewer than $2k$ records which do not belong to the groups formed in Step 3, form a new group with those records and exit the algorithm.

The above algorithm can be applied independently to each group of attributes resulting from partitioning the set of attributes in the data set. In [57], it has been extended to offer better utility for categorical data and in [9] to support attribute values with variable cardinality (set-valued data).

3.3   SYNTHETIC DATA GENERATION

Publication of synthetic—i.e., simulated—data was proposed long ago as a way to guard against statistical disclosure. The idea is to randomly generate data with the constraint that certain statistics or internal relationships of the original data set should be preserved. More than twenty years ago, Rubin suggested in [77] to create an entirely synthetic data set based on the original survey data and multiple imputation. A simulation study of this approach was given in [75].

As stated in 2.5, three types of synthetic data sets are usually considered: (i) fully synthetic data sets [77], where every data item has been synthesized, (ii) partially synthetic data sets [74], where only some variables of some records are synthesized (usually the ones that present a greater risk of disclosure), and (iii) hybrid data sets [19, 65], where the original data is mixed with the synthesized data.

As also stated in 2.5, the generation of fully synthetic data [77] set takes three steps: (i) a model for the population is proposed, (ii) the proposed model is adjusted to the original data set, and (iii) the synthetic data set is generated by drawing from the model (without any further dependency on the original data). The utility of fully synthetic data sets is highly dependent on the accuracy of the adjusted model. If the adjusted model fits well the population, the synthetic data set should be as good as the original data set in terms of statistical analysis power. In this sense, synthetic data are superior in terms of data utility to masking techniques (which always lead to some utility loss).

This advantage of synthetic data is, however, mostly theoretical as (except by the relations between variables that are known in advance) the model must be built from the analysis of the original data. Thus, proposing a model that appropriately captures all the properties of the population is, in general, not feasible: there may be dependencies between variables that are difficult to model or, even, to observe in the original data. Given that only the properties that are included in the model will be present in the synthetic data, it is important to include all the properties of the data that we want to preserve. To reduce the dependency on the models, alternatives to fully synthetic data have been proposed: partially synthetic data and hybrid data. However, using these alternative approaches to reduce the dependency on the model has a cost in terms of risk of disclosure.

As far as the risk of disclosure is concerned, the generation of fully synthetic data is considered to be a very safe approach. Because the synthetic data is generated based solely on the adjusted model, analyzing the risk of disclosure of the synthetic data can be reduced to analyzing the risk of disclosure of the information about the original data that the model incorporates. Because this information is usually reduced to some statistical properties of the original data, disclosure risk is under control. In particular in fully synthetic data, they seem to circumvent the re-identification problem: since published records are invented and do not derive from any original record, it might be concluded that no individual can complain from having been re-identified. At a closer look this advantage is less clear. If, by chance, a published synthetic record matches a particular citizen's non-confidential attributes (age, marital status, place of residence, etc.) and confidential attributes (salary, mortgage, etc.), re-identification using the non-confidential attributes is easy and that citizen may feel that his confidential attributes have been unduly revealed. In that case, the citizen is unlikely to be happy with or even understand the explanation that the record was synthetically generated.

Unlike fully synthetic data, neither partially synthetic nor hybrid data can circumvent re-identification. With partial synthesis, the population units in the original data set are the same population units in the partially synthetic data set. In hybrid data sets the population units in the original data set are present but mixed with synthetic ones.

On the other hand, limited data utility is another problem of synthetic data. Only the statistical properties explicitly captured by the model used by the data protector are preserved. A logical question here is why not directly publish the statistics one wants to preserve rather than release a synthetic microdata set. One possible justification for synthetic microdata would be if valid analyses could be obtained on a number of subdomains, i.e., similar results were obtained in a number of subsets of the original data set and the corresponding subsets of the synthetic data set. Partially synthetic or hybrid microdata are more likely to succeed in staying useful for subdomain analysis. The utility of the synthetic data can be improved by increasing the amount of information that the model includes about the original data. However, this is done at the cost of increasing the risk of disclosure.

See [27] for more background on synthetic data generation.

3.4   SUMMARY

This chapter has reviewed some of the techniques used for disclosure risk limitation in microdata sets. For the non-perturbative masking approach we have discussed: sampling, global recoding, top- and bottom-coding and local suppression. For the perturbative masking approach we have detailed: noise addition, data/rank swapping, and microaggregation. Finally, we have also reviewed synthetic data generation.

CHAPTER 4

Quantifying Disclosure Risk: Record Linkage

Record linkage (a.k.a. data matching or deduplication) was invented to improve data quality when matching files. In the context of anonymization it can be used by the data controller to empirically evaluate the disclosure risk associated with an anonymized data set. The data protector or controller uses a record linkage algorithm (or several such algorithms) to link each record in the anonymized data with a record in the original data set. Since the protector knows the real correspondence between original and protected records, he can determine the percentage of correctly linked pairs, which he uses to estimate the number of re-identifications that might be obtained by a specialized intruder. If the number of re-identifications is too high, the data set needs more anonymization by the controller before it can be released.

In its most basic approach record linkage is based on matching values of shared attributes. All the attributes that are common to both data sets are compared at once. A pair of records is said to match if the common attributes share the same values and they are the only two records sharing those values. A pair of records is said not to match if they differ in the value of some common attribute or if there are multiple pairs of records sharing those same attribute values.

Many times an attribute value may have several valid representations or variations. In that case record linkage based on exact matching of the values of common attributes is not a satisfactory approach. Rather than seeking an exact match between common attributes, a similarity function, sim, between pairs of records is used. For a given pair of records x and y, the similarity function returns a value between 0 and 1 that represents the degree of similarity between the records x and y. It holds that:

- $sim(x, y) \in [0, 1]$. That is, the degree of similarity is in the range $[0, 1]$ with 1 meaning complete similarity and 0 meaning complete dissimilarity.

- $sim(x, y) = 1 \iff x = y$. That is, the similarity is 1 if, and only if, both records are equal.

The similarity function between records can be based on the similarity of the values of common attributes. Thus, the similarity between records can be computed, for instance, as an average or as a weighted average of the similarity of the underlying attributes. As for computing the similarity between attributes several approaches have been proposed. For instance, for categorical data: the edit distance [66] computes the number of insertions, deletions, and substitutions needed to transform one string into the other; [56] proposes a measure to evaluate the semantic similarity between textual values, etc.

4.1 THRESHOLD-BASED RECORD LINKAGE

Threshold-based linkage is the adaptation to similarity functions of attribute matching record linkage. Rather than saying that two records match when the values of all common attributes match, we say that they match when they are similar enough. A threshold is used to determine when two records are similar enough.

When records are to be classified between match and non-match, a single threshold value, t, is enough:

- $sim(x, y) \geq t$: we classify the pair of records x and y as a match.

- $sim(x, y) < t$: we classify the pair of records x and y as a non-match.

The use of a sharp threshold value to distinguish between a match and a non-match may be too narrow-minded. Probably the amount of misclassifications when the similarity is near the threshold value could be large. To avoid this issue an extended classification in three classes is done: match, non-match, and potential match. The match class is used for a pair of records that have been positively identified as a match, the non-match class is used for pair of records that have been positively identified as a non-match, and the class potential match is used for a pair of records that are neither a clear match nor a clear non-match. Classification into the classes match, non-match, and potential match requires the use of two threshold values t_u and t_d (with $t_u > t_d$), used as follows:

- $sim(x, y) \geq t_u$: we classify the pair of records x and y as a match.

- $t_d \leq sim(x, y) \leq t_u$: we classify the pair of records x and y as a potential match.

- $sim(x, y) < t_d$: we classify the pair of records x and y as a non-match.

4.2 RULE-BASED RECORD LINKAGE

Basing the classification on a single value of similarity between records may sometimes be too restrictive. Imagine, for instance, that the data sets contain records related to two types of entities. It may be the case that the way to measure the similarity between records should be done in a different way for the different types of entities. This is not possible if we use a single similarity function.

In rule-based record linkage, we have a vector of similarity functions (e.g., a similarity function for each of the attributes common to both data sets), rather than a single utility function. Then classification rules test several similarity values and output a classification (either match, non-match, or potential match). More formally, a classification rule is a propositional logic formula of the form $P \rightarrow C$, where P test several similarity values combined by the logical operators $\wedge$(and), $\vee$(or), and $\neg$(not), and C is either match, non-match, or potential match. When a rule is triggered for a pair of records (the pair of records satisfy the conditions in P), the outcome of the rule C is used to classify the pair of records.

There are two main approaches to come up with the set of rules: generate them manually based on the domain knowledge of the data sets, or use a supervised learning approach in which pairs of records with the actual classification (match, non-match, or potential match) are passed to the system for it to automatically learn the rules.

4.3   PROBABILISTIC RECORD LINKAGE

Probabilistic record linkage [32, 47] can be seen as an extension of rule-based record linkage in which the outcome of the rules is not a deterministic class in {match, non-match, potential match} but a probability distribution over the three classes. The goal in probabilistic record linkage is to come up with classification mechanisms with predetermined probabilities of misclassification (the error of classifying a pair of records related to the same entity as a non-match and the error of classifying a pair of records related to different entities as a match). Having fixed the probabilities of misclassification, we can consider the set of classification mechanisms that provide these levels of misclassification. Among these, there is one mechanism that has especially good properties and that is known as the *optimal classification mechanism*. The optimal classification mechanism for some given levels of misclassification is the one that has the least probability of outputting potential match. Because pairs of records classified as potential match require further processing (by a potentially costly human expert), the optimal mechanism should be preferred over all the other classification mechanisms with given probabilities of misclassification.

Here we present a slightly simplified version of the original work in probabilistic record linkage [32]. Consider that we have two sets of entities X and Y that are, in principle, not disjoint. That is, a given entity can be present in both X and Y. The data sets are generated as a randomized function of the original data that accounts for the possible variations and errors of the record corresponding to an entity: for $x \in X$ the corresponding record is $\alpha(x)$ and for $y \in Y$ the corresponding record $\beta(y)$. Thus, even if $x = y$, it may be $\alpha(x) \neq \beta(y)$ and even if $x \neq y$, it may be $\alpha(x) = \beta(y)$.

We use $\alpha(X)$ and $\beta(Y)$ to represent the data sets to be linked. Linking $\alpha(X)$ and $\beta(Y)$ implies considering each pair of records of $\alpha(X) \times \beta(Y)$ and classifying it as either a match, a non-match, or a potential match. The set $\alpha(X) \times \beta(Y)$ can be split into two parts: the set of real matches

$$M = \{(\alpha(x), \beta(y)) : x = y\},$$

and the set of real non-matches

$$U = \{(\alpha(x), \beta(y)) : x \neq y\}.$$

Of course, *ex ante* determining the actual contents of M and U is not possible; otherwise, there would be no need for a record linkage methodology.

Like in rule-based record linkage, the first step to determine if two records should be linked is to compute a vector of similarity functions. We define the similarity vector for $\alpha(x)$ and $\beta(y)$ as

$$\gamma(\alpha(x), \beta(y)) = (\gamma^1(\alpha(x), \beta(y)), \dots, \gamma^k(\alpha(x), \beta(y))).$$

Even though we have used $\gamma(\alpha(x), \beta(y))$ to emphasize that the vector is computed over pairs of records of $\alpha(X) \times \beta(Y)$, it should be noted that the domain of γ is $X \times Y$. The set of possible realizations of γ is called the comparison space and is denoted by Γ.

For a given realization $\gamma_0 \in \Gamma$ we are interested in two conditional probabilities: the probability of getting γ_0 given a real match, $P(\gamma_0|M)$, and the probability of γ_0 given a real non-match, $P(\gamma_0|U)$. With these probabilities we can compute the *agreement ratio* of γ_0:

$$R(\gamma_0) = \frac{P(\gamma_0|M)}{P(\gamma_0|U)}.$$

During the linkage we observe $\gamma(\alpha(x), \beta(y))$ and have to decide whether $(\alpha(x), \beta(y)) \in M$ (classify it as a match) or $(\alpha(x), \beta(y)) \in U$ (classify it as a non-match). To account for the cases in which the decision between match and non-match is not clear, we also allow the classification of $(\alpha(x), \beta(y))$ as a potential match. A linkage rule is used for the classification of the pair $(\alpha(x), \beta(y))$ based on the similarity vector. Thus, a linkage rule is a mapping between Γ (the comparison space) to a probability distribution over the possible classifications: match (L), non-match (N), and potential match (C).

$$\mathcal{L} : \Gamma \to \{(p_L, p_N, p_C) \in [0, 1]^3 : p_L + p_N + p_C = 1\}.$$

Of course, a linkage rule need not always give the correct classification. A false match is a linked pair that is not a real match. A false non-match is a non-linked pair that is a real match. Thus, a rule can be tagged with the probability of false matches, $\mu = P_{\mathcal{L}}(L|U)$, and with the probability of false non-matches, $\lambda = P_{\mathcal{L}}(N|M)$.

In [32] an optimal linkage rule is presented. The rule is optimal in the sense that for maximum tolerable probabilities of misclassification μ and λ, the rule has the least probability of outputting a potential match. This rule is based on thresholding the agreement ratio. It classifies each possible similarity vector in Γ into match, non-match, or potential match according to the agreement ratio. Given a pair of records $(\alpha(a), \beta(b))$, the similarity vector $\gamma(\alpha(x), \beta(y))$ is computed and the classification is given by the rule:

$$\begin{cases} R(\gamma(\alpha(x), \beta(y))) \geq T_\mu & \rightarrow match \\ R(\gamma(\alpha(x), \beta(y))) \leq T_\lambda & \rightarrow non-match \\ T_\lambda < R(\gamma(\alpha(x), \beta(y))) < T_\mu & \rightarrow potential \end{cases}$$

where T_μ and T_λ are upper and lower threshold values. The error rates for this rule are:

$$\mu = \sum_{\gamma \in \Gamma: R(\gamma) \geq T_\mu} P(\gamma|U).$$

$$\lambda = \sum_{\gamma \in \Gamma: R(\gamma) \leq T_\lambda} P(\gamma|M).$$

4.4   SUMMARY

This chapter has introduced record linkage. Record linkage is a technique that can be used by an intruder, for instance, to try to re-identify the records in a published data set. On the other hand, record linkage can also be used by the data publisher for disclosure risk assessment prior to data release. The data publisher simulates an intruder by running a record linkage on the data set to be released and checking the proportion of records that are correctly re-identified. Regarding the techniques used to perform record linkage, we have presented a basic approach (based on matching the value of the common attributes) and several more elaborated approaches: threshold-based record linkage, rule-based record linkage, and probabilistic record linkage. In addition to the references given in the chapter, a survey on record linkage can be found in [102].

CHAPTER 5

The k-Anonymity Privacy Model

k-anonymity is a popular privacy model for microdata releases. It seeks to prevent re-identification of records based on a predefined set of (quasi-identifier) attributes, thereby preserving the anonymity of the respondents in the data set. Although the privacy guarantees offered by k-anonymity are limited (i.e., it does not protect against attribute disclosure), its simplicity has made it quite popular. It is sometimes seen as offering a minimal requirement for disclosure risk limitation that is later complemented with protection against attribute disclosure.

5.1 INSUFFICIENCY OF DATA DE-IDENTIFICATION

Data de-identification, that is, removal of the explicit identifiers from records in the data set, is a necessary step to protect the anonymity of the respondents in a microdata release. However, mere de-identification is not sufficient to guarantee anonymity. The released data often contain attributes (such as age, sex, ZIP code, etc.) whose combination makes a record unique and, thus, can lead to its re-identification (successful attribution of an identity to the record). This re-identification is done by linking the attributes in the released data set to an externally available data set containing identifiers.

A clarifying analysis of the potential impact of demographic attributes on the anonymity of individuals is presented in [35]. Based on the U.S. 2000 census, [35] analyzes the anonymity of individuals based on three demographic attributes: date of birth, sex, and location. The following table shows the percentage of individuals that can be uniquely re-identified according to the level of detail of the date of birth and the location.

Birth date	5-digit ZIP	County
Year	0.2%	0.0%
Year and month	4.2%	0.2%
Year, month, and day	63.3%	14.8%

The amount of externally available information together with the increasing amounts of computational power facilitate conducting such re-identifications. In fact, several well-known cases of disclosure have occurred that corroborate this.

The Group Insurance Commission Case

The Group Insurance Commission (GIC) is in charge of buying health care insurance for Massachusetts state employees. In the development of this task the GIC collected in each encounter, among other attributes, the ZIP code, birth date, sex, visit date, diagnosis, procedure, medication, and total charge. Because of the lack of direct identifiers among these attributes, the data were believed to be anonymous and released to researchers and to the industry. On the other hand, the voter registration list for Cambridge (Massachusetts) is accessible at a small fee. Among other attributes, it contains the ZIP code, birth date, sex, name, and address.

The non-de-identified data in the voter registration list can be linked to the medical information by using the attributes they share: ZIP code, birth date, and sex. In this way, an identity can be attributed to some of the records in the medical data set. This approach was used to re-identify medical records belonging to William Weld, a former governor of Massachusetts [100].

The AOL Case

In their interaction with web search engines, users may reveal confidential information. All the information gathered from a user is used by the web search engine to build an individualized profile of her. This profile is not only used by the web search engine to refine forthcoming searches but also to perform targeted advertising or even to sell profiles to third parties.

In 2006 AOL, instead of keeping the collected data for internal use, released a search log containing over 20 million searches performed by 657,426 users. In an attempt to preserve the privacy of the individuals in the data set, AOL replaced the names of the users with numbers. However, two reporters from the *New York Times*, Michael Barbaro and Tom Zeller [7], showed how easily a number can be tracked down to a real identity.

User number 4,417,749 had conducted several hundreds of queries on several topics such as "60 single men," "dog that urinates on everything," "landscapers in Lilburn," and several people with the last name "Arnold." The *New York Times* reporters were able to track down these queries to Thelma Arnold. When interviewed by the reporters Thelma said: "My goodness, it's my whole personal life. I had no idea that somebody was looking over my shoulder."

AOL removed the access to the released search log but copies of it still circulate.

5.2   THE k-ANONYMITY MODEL

k-anonymity [79, 80] seeks to guarantee a minimum level of anonymity for the records in a data set. k-anonymity assumes that the set of attributes that an intruder can use to re-identify a record are known, and makes each record indistinguishable with regard to these attributes within a group of k records.

A quasi-identifier is a set of attributes whose combination of values can lead to record re-identification and, hence, its release must be controlled. Recall that, when describing microdata sets in Section 2.2, we used the term "quasi-identifier attribute" to refer to attributes that can be used in record re-identification. These notions are related but are not equivalent. The attributes that conform a quasi-identifier are quasi-identifier attributes, but a quasi-identifier attribute alone does not need to be a quasi-identifier. Let X be a data set with attributes $X^1, \ldots, X^m$. Let us use QI_X to refer to the set of quasi-identifiers associated with X.

Whether a combination of attributes should be considered to be a quasi-identifier depends on the available external information with identifiers. The set of quasi-identifiers usually encompasses all the combinations of attributes that the data releaser reasonably considers to be publicly available in a non-de-identified data set. However, unless each combination of attributes is defined to be a quasi-identifier, it would be difficult for the data anonymizer to argue that no other combination of attributes could be used for record re-identification. Some intruders may be in possession of confidential information or data that were not public at the time of anonymization and could be made publicly available later.

To prevent re-identification of records based on a quasi-identifier, k-anonymity requires each combination of values of the quasi-identifier attributes to be shared by k or more records.

Definition 5.1 k-anonymity   Let X be a data set with attributes $X^1, \ldots, X^m$. Let $QI \in QI_X$ be a quasi-identifier. X is said to be k-anonymous if each combination of values of the attributes in QI that appears in X is shared by k or more records. Although we have defined QI_X to be the set of all quasi-identifiers of X, the notion of k-anonymity is restricted to a single quasi-identifier $QI \in QI_X$. The usual assumption is that several k-anonymous versions of X can be released to different target recipients. Each target recipient r is assumed to have a single quasi-identifier $QI_r \in QI_X$ that is used for the generation of the k-anonymous data for r. Be aware, however, that if any recipient has access to the k-anonymous data set tailored for another recipient, disclosure may happen. To generate a k-anonymous data set that offers protection against re-identification based on either of the quasi-identifiers $QI_1, \ldots, QI_s \in QI_X$ the union quasi-identifier $QI_1 \cup \ldots \cup QI_s$ must be considered.

Definition 5.2   Equivalence class   The equivalence class of a record $x \in X$ for a given quasi-identifier in $QI \in QI_X$ is the set of records in X sharing with x the values for all the attributes in QI. Using the notion of equivalence class, the definition of k-anonymity can be rephrased as follows: a data set is k-anonymous if and only if the equivalence class of any record has k or more records.

To illustrate the concepts introduced until now and to help in further developing k-anonymity we introduce a sample data set containing medical data. Table 5.1 shows the sample medical data set containing one identifying attribute (SS number), two quasi-identifier attributes (Age and ZIP code) and one confidential attribute (Condition). Table 5.2 shows a possible anonymized version of the data set satisfying 4-anonymity. The identifier attribute has been removed, because it allows direct re-identification of each record. The amount of information in the quasi-identifiers has been reduced to make them less identifying. Each combination of values of quasi-identifiers is now shared by at least four records. To reduce the information in the quasi-identifiers we have used generalization. Essentially, we have replaced each of the original values by ranges.

Table 5.1: Sample medical data set with identifier, quasi-identifier, and confidential attributes

	Identifier	Quasi-identifiers		Confidential
	SS Number	**Age**	**ZIP code**	**Condition**
1	1234-12-1234	21	23058	Heart Disease
2	2345-23-2345	24	23059	Heart Disease
3	3456-34-3456	26	23060	Viral Infection
4	4567-45-4567	27	23061	Viral Infection
5	5678-56-5678	43	23058	Kidney Stone
6	6789-67-6789	43	23059	Heart Disease
7	7890-78-7890	47	23060	Viral Infection
8	8901-89-8901	49	23061	Viral Infection
9	9012-90-9012	32	23058	Kidney Stone
10	0123-12-0123	34	23059	Kidney Stone
11	4321-43-4321	35	23060	AIDS
12	5432-54-5432	38	23061	AIDS

k-anonymity, like other privacy models, states the conditions that the released data must satisfy for disclosure risk to be under control. However, it does not specify the method that must be used to attain such conditions. Thus, the 4-anonymous data set in Table 5.2 could have been generated using methods other than generalization. Of course, the resulting 4-anonymous data set would have been different. Two dominant approaches exist to generate k-anonymous data sets: the first one is based on generalization and suppression, and the second one is based on (multivariate) microaggregation.

Table 5.2: 4-anonymous medical data generated by generalization (global recoding)

| | Identifier | Quasi-identifiers | | Confidential |
	SS Number	Age	ZIP code	Condition
1	*	[20-30]	230**	Heart Disease
2	*	[20-30]	230**	Heart Disease
3	*	[20-30]	230**	Viral Infection
4	*	[20-30]	230**	Viral Infection
5	*	[40-50]	230**	Kidney Stone
6	*	[40-50]	230**	Heart Disease
7	*	[40-50]	230**	Viral Infection
8	*	[40-50]	230**	Viral Infection
9	*	[30-40]	230**	Kidney Stone
10	*	[30-40]	230**	Kidney Stone
11	*	[30-40]	230**	AIDS
12	*	[30-40]	230**	AIDS

5.3 GENERALIZATION AND SUPPRESSION BASED k-ANONYMITY

The domain of an attribute specifies the values that the attribute can take. In order to attain k-anonymity, generalization reduces the amount of information in the attribute values. This is done by mapping the original values of the attributes to generalized versions. Usually several generalizations are possible for each attribute. These generalizations are related and form a generalization hierarchy.

In one-dimensional generalization, each attribute is generalized independently. To that end, we assume that a domain generalization hierarchy is available for each attribute. Figure 5.1 shows a possible generalization hierarchy for the Age attribute: in *Age0* the original, ungeneralized values of the attribute are present, in *Age1* the original values have been replaced by intervals of size 5, in *Age2* the intervals in *Age3* are grouped to form intervals of size 10, and in *Age3* there is a single interval that contains all the original values. Figure 5.2 shows a possible generalization hierarchy for ZIP code: in *Zip0* the original, ungeneralized values of the attribute are present, in *Zip1* the last figure of the ZIP code is left undetermined, and in *Zip2* the last two figures of the ZIP code are left undetermined. We observe in both cases that the various generalizations of each attribute are related according to a generalization relationship: *Age3* is more general than *Age2*, which is in turn more general than *Age1*, which in turn is more general than *Age0*.

Definition 5.3 Attribute generalization relationship Consider an attribute X^i of the data set X. Let G_1 and G_2 be two possible generalizations of the domain of the attribute X^i. We denote the attribute generalization relationship $\leq_{X^i}$. We use the notation $G_1 \leq_{X^i} G_2$ to denote that the G_2 is either identical or a generalization of G_1. The generalization relationship $\leq_{X^i}$ defines a partial order between the generalizations of X^i. By following the usual approach to attribute generalization for k-anonymity, we assume that $\leq_{X^i}$ is a total order. Although this requirement would not be necessary, it will facilitate the exposition. With a total order, for each attribute X^i we have a linear sequence of generalizations of the form $G_0^i \leq_{X^i} G_1^i \leq_{X^i} \ldots \leq_{X^i} G_{h_i}^i$ where G_0^i is the domain of the original attribute and $G_{h_i}^i$ is the generalization into a single value.

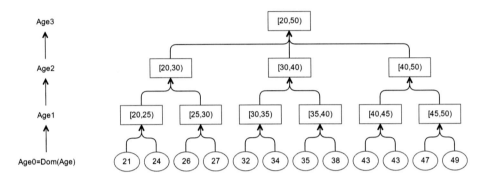

Figure 5.1: Generalization hierarchy for the Age attribute. At the bottom, Age_0, represents the original (non-generalized) domain of the attribute. The first generalization, Age_1, replaces the original values by ranges of length 5. The second generalization, Age_2, considers ranges of ages of size 10. The last generalization, Age_3, groups all age values in a single category.

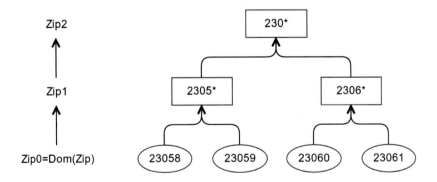

Figure 5.2: Generalization hierarchy for the ZIP code attribute. At the bottom, Zip_0, represents the original (ungeneralized) domain of the attribute. The first generalization, Zip_1, groups ZIP codes whose first four figures match. The second generalization, Zip_2, groups all ZIP codes in the data set.

Once the generalization hierarchies have been defined for each individual attribute, we combine them to get a record generalization (that is, we select a generalization for each attribute).

Definition 5.4   Record generalization   Let X be a data set with attributes $X^1, \ldots, X^m$. A record generalization is a tuple $(G_1, \ldots, G_m)$ where G_i is a generalization of the domain of attribute X^i. We will implicitly assume that, for a given data set, record generalizations are performed on the projection on the quasi-identifiers. Like in the case of a single attribute, a partial order can be defined between record generalizations.

Definition 5.5   Record generalization relationship   Let X be a data set with attributes $X^1, \ldots, X^m$. Let $(G_1, \ldots, G_m)$ and $(G'_1, \ldots, G'_m)$ be two record generalizations. We denote the record generalization relationship by $\leq_X$ and we use the notation $(G_1, \ldots, G_m) \leq_X (G'_1, \ldots, G'_m)$ to indicate that G'_i is either identical or a generalization of G_i, for each $i = 1, \ldots, m$.

The goal is to select a record generalization so that k-anonymity is satisfied. In the generation of a k-anonymous data set, only the quasi-identifier attributes are generalized; we will restrict the generalizations to them. There are potentially many different generalizations that yield k-anonymity. Because the level of generalization is directly related to the amount of information loss, the goal is to find the minimal generalization.

Definition 5.6   Minimal record generalization for k-anonymity   Let X be a data set with attributes $X^1, \ldots, X^m$. Let QI be the quasi-identifier attributes and let G be a record generalization over QI. We say that G is a minimal record generalization if it satisfies k-anonymity and, for any other record generalization G' over QI with $G' \leq_{QI} G$, we have that G' does not satisfy k-anonymity. In other words, according to $\leq_{QI}$, G is minimal among the record generalizations over QI that satisfy k-anonymity.

Figure 5.3 shows the possible record generalizations for Age and ZIP according to the previously given generalization hierarchies for the individual attributes. The valid combinations of attribute generalizations to attain 2-anonymity are: (Age_3, Zip_2), (Age_3, Zip_1), (Age_3, Zip_0), (Age_2, Zip_2), (Age_2, Zip_1), (Age_1, Zip_2), (Age_1, Zip_1). These are marked with a rectangle in the figure. Among the attribute generalizations that satisfy 2-anonymity the minimal ones are: (Age_3, Zip_0) and (Age_1, Zip_1).

Not all minimal generalizations are equally good. For example, if in Figure 5.3 we are interested in preserving the ZIP code information as much as possible, the generalization selected should be $(Age3, Zip0)$. On the contrary, if we are interested in minimizing the total number of generalization steps, we should select $(Age1, Zip1)$: $(Age1, Zip1)$ generalizes each attribute once, thus making a total of two generalizations steps, while $(Age3, Zip0)$ involves three generalization steps.

Coming up with the minimal record generalization that is optimal according to some criterion requires finding the set of all minimal generalizations and searching the optimal one among them. Given the large number of record generalizations ($(h_1 + \ldots + h_{|QI|})! / h_1! \ldots h_{|QI|}!$, where h_i is the

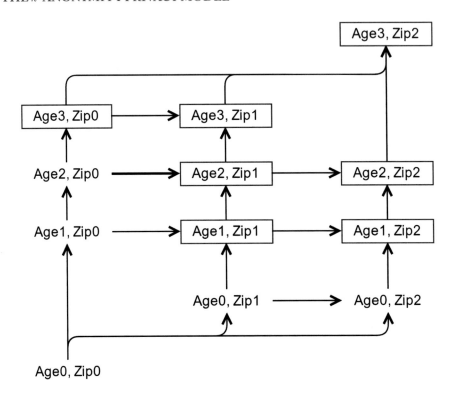

Figure 5.3: Possible combinations of domain generalizations of attributes Age and ZIP code. The rectangles mark the combinations of generalizations that satisfy 2-anonymity.

number of generalizations for attribute QI^i), finding the set of minimal generalizations can be intractable and may require strategies to reduce the search space. We review next some well-known algorithms for this purpose.

Minimizing the height of the generalization
This was the original method to generate a k-anonymous data set [79]. It finds a minimal generalization that minimizes the number of generalization steps (height of the generalization).

Definition 5.7 Height of a generalization   Let X be a data set with attributes $X^1, \ldots, X^m$. Let $G_0^i \leq_{X^i} G_1^i \leq_{X^i} \ldots \leq_{X^i} G_{h_i}^i$ be the sequence of generalizations for attribute X^i. We define the height of G_j^i as

$$height(G_j^i) = j.$$

The height of a record generalization $(G_{i_1}^1, \ldots, G_{i_m}^m)$ is defined as

$$height((G_{i_1}^1, \ldots, G_{i_m}^m)) = i_1 + \ldots + i_m.$$

The height of a record generalization is between 0 and $h_1 + \ldots + h_m$. The proposed algorithm is based on a binary search over the height of the record generalizations. If, for a given height h, there is no record generalization satisfying k-anonymity, then there cannot be a record generalization at a lower height that satisfies k-anonymity. Thus, if no record generalization satisfying k-anonymity is found at height h, there is no need to check the record generalizations at height lower than h. On the contrary, if a record generalization that satisfies k-anonymity is found at height h, then the record generalizations at height higher than h are not minimal and can be discarded. See Algorithm 2 for a formal description of the process.

The Incognito algorithm

Algorithm 2 was effective in finding a solution because the optimality criterion (minimizing the height of the generalization) was compatible with a binary search based on the height (in the sense that if, for a given height there is no record generalization that gives k-anonymity, then there is no need to check record generalizations with a lower height). However, this does not need to be the case for an arbitrary optimality criterion. In such case a naive bottom-up breadth-first search algorithm may need to be used.

The Incognito algorithm follows the bottom-up breadth-first approach to find the optimal record generalization. To be able to limit the search space, the Incognito algorithm uses the following properties about generalizations and k-anonymity.

Proposition 5.8 Generalization property   Let X be a data set, let QI be the quasi-identifier attributes of X, and let G_1 and G_2 be record generalizations over QI such that $G_1 \leq_{QI} G_2$. If G_1 gives k-anonymity to X, then G_2 also gives k-anonymity to X.

Proposition 5.9 Rollup property   Let X be a data set, let QI be the quasi-identifier attributes of X, and let G_1 and G_2 be record generalizations over QI such that $G_1 \leq_{QI} G_2$. The frequency count of a given equivalence class $\mathcal{C}$ in X with respect to G_2 can be computed as the sum of the frequency counts of the equivalence classes in X with respect to G_1 that generalize to $\mathcal{C}$.

Proposition 5.10 Subset property   Let X be a data set, let QI be the quasi-identifier attributes of X, and let $Q \subset QI$ be a subset of the quasi-identifiers. If X is k-anonymous with respect to Q, then it is also k-anonymous with respect to any subset of attributes of Q.

The subset property says that for a given generalization to satisfy k-anonymity, all the generalizations that result by removing one of the attributes must also satisfy k-anonymity. Based on this, the Incognito algorithm starts by searching for single attribute generalizations that give

---

Algorithm 2 k-Anonymous record generalization with minimal height

---

Data: X: original data set

   k: anonymity requirement

   QI: quasi-identifier attributes

   $(G_j^i)_j$: generalization hierarchy for attribute QI^i, for all $i = 1, \dots, |QI|$

Result: Set of clusters satisfying k-anonymity and t-closeness

$low := 0; high := h_1 + \dots + h_{|QI|}$

$sol = (G_{h_1}^1, \dots, G_{h_{|QI|}}^{|QI|})$

while $low < high$ **do**

  $mid := \left\lfloor \frac{low+high}{2} \right\rfloor$

  $generalizations := \{(G_{i_i}^1, \dots, G_{i_{|QI|}}^{|QI|}) | height((G_{i_i}^1, \dots, G_{i_{|QI|}}^{|QI|})) = mid\}$

  $found :=$**false**

  while $generalizations \neq \emptyset$ **and** $found \neq$**true do**

    Extract $(G_1, \dots, G_{|QI|})$ from $generalizations$

    if $(G_1, \dots, G_{|QI|})$ satisfies k-anonymity **then**

      $sol = (G_1, \dots, G_{|QI|})$

      $found :=$**true**

    end if

  end while

  if $found =$**true then**

    $high := mid$

  else

    $low := mid + 1$

  end if

end while

return sol

---

k-anonymity and then iteratively increases the number of attributes in the generalization by one. When searching for the generalizations of size i that satisfy k-anonymity, the Incognito algorithm makes use of the generalization property to reduce the search space: once a generalization G that satisfies k-anonymity is found, all further generalizations of G also satisfy k-anonymity. To reduce the cost of checking whether the frequency counts associated with a generalization satisfy k-anonymity, the Incognito algorithm makes use of the rollup property and computes the frequency counts associated to a generalization in terms of the already computed frequency counts for the previous generalizations. Algorithm 3 shows the formal description of the Incognito algorithm.

Algorithm 3 Incognito algorithm for k-anonymity

Data: X: original data set

$\qquad$ k: anonymity requirement

$\qquad$ QI: quasi-identifier attributes

$\qquad$ $(G_j^i)_j$: generalization hierarchy for attribute QI^i, for all $i = 1, \ldots, |QI|$

Result: Set of record generalizations that yield k-anonymity

$C_1 :=$ {Nodes in the generalization hierarchies of the attributes in QI}

$E_1 :=$ {Edges in the generalization hierarchies of the attributes in QI}

queue :=empty queue

for $i := 1, \ldots, |QI|$ **do**

$\qquad$ //S_i will contain all the generalizations with i attributes that are k-anonymous

$\qquad$ $S_i := C_1$

$\qquad$ *roots* :=nodes of C_i with no incoming edge

$\qquad$ Insert *roots* into *queue* and keep it sorted by height

$\qquad$ **while** *queue* $\neq \emptyset$ **do**

$\qquad\qquad$ *node* :=extract item from *queue*

$\qquad\qquad$ **if** *node* is not tagged **then**

$\qquad\qquad\qquad$ **if** *node* $\in$ *roots* **then**

$\qquad\qquad\qquad\qquad$ *frequencies* :=compute frequencies of T with respect to *node*

$\qquad\qquad\qquad$ **else**

$\qquad\qquad\qquad\qquad$ *frequencies* :=compute frequencies of T with respect to *node* using parent's frequency

$\qquad\qquad\qquad$ **end if**

$\qquad\qquad$ **end if**

$\qquad\qquad$ Check for k-anonymity of X with respect to *node* using *frequencies*

$\qquad\qquad$ **if** X is k-anonymous with respect to *node* **then**

$\qquad\qquad\qquad$ tag all direct generalizations of *node*

$\qquad\qquad$ **else**

$\qquad\qquad\qquad$ Delete *node* from S_i

$\qquad\qquad\qquad$ Insert direct generalizations of *node* into *queue* and keep the order by height

$\qquad\qquad$ **end if**

$\qquad$ **end while**

$\qquad$ //Generate the graph of all possible k-anonymous generalizations with $i + 1$ attributes

$\qquad$ $C_{i+1}, E_{i+1} :=$Generate graph from S_i and E_i

end for

return S_n

5.4   MICROAGGREGATION-BASED k-ANONYMITY

Satisfying k-anonymity with minimal data modification by using generalization (recoding) and local suppression has been shown to be NP-hard. In fact, even how to optimally combine generalization and local suppression is an open issue. Unless carefully combined, those two non-perturbative methods may cause a substantial loss of data utility. Furthermore, the use of generalization to ensure k-anonymity poses several practical problems. One of them is the computational cost of finding the optimal recoding. This is partly related to the exponential number of generalizations that can be defined for each attribute.

Lemma 5.11   For an attribute with c categories, there are $2^c - c - 1$ possible generalizations.

Proof. Generalization consists of replacing a subset of categories by a new general category. Thus the number of generalizations equals the number of subsets of categories containing more than one category. There are 2^c subsets of categories, of which c consist of a single category and one is the empty subset. Thus there are $2^c - c - 1$ subsets containing more than one category.   □

Another problem is determining the subset of appropriate generalizations, i.e., which are the new categories and which is the subset of old categories that can be recoded into each of such new categories. Not all recoding methods are appropriate because the semantics of the categories and the intended data uses must be taken into account. For example, when generalizing ZIP codes, recoding 08201 and 08205 into 0820* makes sense as long as 0820* is meaningful as a location (e.g., corresponds to a city, a county, or another geographical area). For the same reason, it is probably not meaningful to recode 08201 and 05201 into 0*201 because the set of regions represented by 0*201 might lack any geographical significance. The need for significance makes automatic generation of recodings a thorny issue.

In comparison, microaggregation stands out as a seamless approach to satisfy k-anonymity. The use of multivariate microaggregation as a masking technique to attain k-anonymity was proposed in [26] (see Section 3.2 for the detailed algorithm). There, microaggregation is performed on the projection on quasi-identifier attributes to generate a k-anonymous data set. The adaptation of microaggregation for k-anonymity is straightforward: by applying the multivariate microaggregation algorithm (with minimum cluster size k) to the quasi-identifiers, one generates groups of k records that share the quasi-identifier values (the aggregation step replaces the original quasi-identifiers by the cluster centroid). In microaggregation one seeks to maximize the homogeneity of records within a cluster, which is beneficial for the utility of the resultant k-anonymous data set. Even if optimal multivariate microaggregation is also NP-hard [70]—like generalization/suppression—near-optimal heuristics exist, unlike for generalization/suppression.

Microaggregation has several advantages over generalization/recoding for k-anonymity that are mostly related to data utility preservation:

- Global recoding may recode some records that do not need it, hence causing extra information loss. On the other hand, local recoding makes data analysis more complex, as values corresponding to various different levels of generalization may co-exist in the anonymized data. Microaggregation is free from either drawback.

• Data generalization usually results in a significant loss of granularity, because input values can only be replaced by a reduced set of generalizations, which are more constrained as one moves up in the hierarchy. Microaggregation, on the other hand, does not reduce the granularity of values, because they are replaced by numerical or categorical averages.

• If outliers are present in the input data, the need to generalize them results in very coarse generalizations and, thus, in a high loss of information. For microaggregation, the influence of an outlier in the calculation of averages/centroids is restricted to the outlier's equivalence class and hence is less noticeable.

• For numerical attributes, generalization discretizes input numbers to numerical ranges and thereby changes the nature of data from continuous to discrete. In contrast, microaggregation maintains the continuous nature of numbers.

In [79, 80] it was proposed to combine local suppression with recoding to reduce the amount of recoding. Local suppression has several drawbacks:

• It is not known how to optimally combine generalization and local suppression.

• There is no agreement in the literature on how suppression should be performed: one can suppress at the record level (entire record suppressed), or suppress particular attributes in some records; furthermore, suppression can be done by either blanking a value or replacing it by a neutral value (i.e., some kind of average).

• Last but not least, and no matter how suppression is performed, it complicates data analysis (users need to resort to software dealing with censored data).

5.5   PROBABILISTIC k-ANONYMITY

k-anonymity guarantees that, for any combination of values of quasi-identifier attributes in the published microdata set Y, there are at least k records sharing that combination of values. Given an individual in an external non-anonymous data set, we cannot link her back to a specific record in Y but to an equivalence class. Thus, the probability of performing the right re-identification is at most $1/k$.

The essence of the anonymity guarantee provided by k-anonymity is to limit the probability of record re-identification to $1/k$. Having at least k records that share the same values for the quasi-identifier attributes is one way to limit the probability of re-identification to $1/k$. However, there may be other approaches to limit this probability.

Probabilistic k-anonymity [90, 95] is a relaxation of k-anonymity that just focuses on offering a probability $1/k$ of record re-identification.

Definition 5.12   Probabilistic k-anonymity   Let X be a data set with attributes $X^1, \ldots, X^m$. Let $QI \in QI_X$ be a quasi-identifier. X is said to satisfy probabilistic k-anonymity with respect to QI if the probability of re-identifying a record based on the QI attributes is, at most, $1/k$.

The main advantage of probabilistic k-anonymity over k-anonymity is that the former does not specify the approach to attain the required limit in the probability of record re-identification. By widening the range of usable methods, one can hope to find a method incurring less information loss.

Proposition 5.13   Let X be a data set with attributes $X^1, \ldots, X^m$. Let $QI \in QI_X$ be a quasi-identifier. If X satisfies k-anonymity with respect to QI, then it satisfies probabilistic k-anonymity with respect to QI. On the contrary, probabilistic k-anonymity with respect to QI does not imply k-anonymity with respect to QI.

Because probabilistic k-anonymity is a relaxation of k-anonymity, in general k-anonymity implies probabilistic k-anonymity, but the reverse does not hold. In this way, the set of methods available to attain probabilistic k-anonymity is a superset of the ones that yield k-anonymity; hence, it is reasonable to expect that probabilistic k-anonymity can be satisfied with less utility damage than k-anonymity.

An interesting manner of attaining probabilistic k-anonymity is proposed in [107]. This method, called Anatomy, simply partitions the original data set in groups of k or more records and then outputs two separate tables for release: one contains the QI attributes together with the group identifier, and the other contains the sensitive attributes together with the group identifier. Because the relation between the QI attributes and the sensitive attributes goes through the group identifiers, the probability of doing the right matching (and thus of re-identifying the confidential attributes) is, at most, $1/k$. The advantage of the Anatomy approach over methods used to attain k-anonymity is that the original values of the QI attributes are preserved and, thus, there is less information loss.

In [90, 95], it is shown that conducting an individual-ranking microaggregation for each confidential attribute leads to a probabilistically k-anonymous data set. As stated in Section 3.2, using individual-ranking microaggregation (instead of the multivariate microaggregation required by k-anonymity) significantly improves the utility of the anonymized data. This becomes more noticeable as the number of quasi-identifiers grows: such curse of dimensionality [6] has only a marginal effect when using univariate microaggregation.

5.6   SUMMARY

This chapter has reviewed the k-anonymity, a privacy model for microdata releases that seeks to prevent record re-identification by making each record indistinguishable within as group of k (or more) records as far as the quasi-identifiers are concerned. We have seen that two main approaches to generate k-anonymous data sets are used in practice: the first one is based on generalization and suppression, and the second one on microaggregation. We have also introduced probabilistic k-anonymity, a relaxation of k-anonymity that seeks to preserve the anonymity guarantees of k-anonymity but with less information loss. The next chapter details two extensions of k-anonymity that focus on protecting against attribute disclosure: l-diversity and t-closeness.

CHAPTER 6

Beyond k-Anonymity: l-Diversity and t-Closeness

The main advantage of k-anonymity is that it provides an intuitive notion of disclosure risk limitation. The principle that underlies k-anonymity is that an individual's privacy must be protected if the corresponding record is hidden within a group of k records. However, this principle fails to provide sufficient protection when the records in the k-anonymous group have a similar value for the confidential attribute. In other words, k-anonymity provides protection against identity disclosure but that is not enough to prevent attribute disclosure when the values of the confidential attribute are similar across records.

Two simple attacks have been proposed in the literature that exploit the lack of variability in the confidential attribute. In the homogeneity attack, all the records in a k-anonymous group share the same value for the confidential attribute; thus, k-anonymity fails to provide any protection against attribute disclosure. In the background knowledge attack, the variability of the confidential attribute in the k-anonymous group is small and the intruder is in possession of some background information that allows her to further restrict the feasible values of the confidential attribute for the target individual.

6.1 l-DIVERSITY

In an attempt to overcome the issues that k-anonymity presents against attribute disclosure, [54] proposes the notion of l-diversity. The goal is to require a minimum level of diversity for the confidential attribute in each of the k-anonymous groups of records (i.e., equivalence classes).

Definition 6.1 l**-diversity [54]** An equivalence class is said to satisfy l-diversity if there are at least l "well-represented" values for the sensitive attribute. A data set is said to satisfy l-diversity if every equivalence class in it satisfies l-diversity.

The definition of l-diversity is vague in the sense that it does not specify the meaning of "well-represented" values. Some possible interpretations are:

1. Distinct l-diversity. This is the simplest notion of l-diversity. It only requires each equivalence class to have at least l different values for the sensitive attribute. This is indeed a weak instantiation of the l-diversity principle as the frequency of the values of the sensitive attribute could be significantly different.

2. Entropy l-diversity. The entropy of an equivalence class S is

$$H(S) = -\sum_{s \in S} p_S(s) \log(p_S(s))$$

where $p_S(s)$ is the fraction of records in the equivalence class S with sensitive value equal to s. A table is said to satisfy entropy l-diversity if, for each equivalence class S, we have

$$H(S) \geq \log l.$$

This instantiation of l-diversity may be too restrictive if some values of the sensitive attribute are very common because, in such cases, the entropy of equivalence classes tends to be small.

3. Recursive (c, l)-diversity. This instantiation seeks to upper-bound the frequency of the most common value of the sensitive attribute and lower-bound the frequency of the least common values. Assuming that $r_1, \ldots, r_m$ is the sequence of frequencies of the values of the sensitive attribute in an equivalence class in descending order, we say the the class satisfies (c, l)-diversity if

$$r_1 < c(r_l + r_{l+1} + \ldots + r_m).$$

6.2 t-CLOSENESS

l-diversity tries to mitigate the risk of attribute disclosure by requiring a minimal level of variability in the sensitive attribute in each equivalence class. However, the formulation of l-diversity is not completely satisfactory as it is vulnerable to skewness and and similarity attacks [50].

- *Skewness attack.* To give the least amount of information about the sensitive attribute on a particular individual, l-diversity seeks to make the frequency of appearance of each these values similar in each equivalence class. However, when the distribution of the sensitive attribute in the overall data set is strongly skewed, satisfying l-diversity may in fact be counter-productive as far as disclosure risk is concerned. Consider the case of a medical data set in which the sensitive attribute records the presence or absence of a given disease. Assume that 99% of the individuals are negative. Releasing an equivalence class with 50% positives and 50% negatives is optimal in terms of l-diversity but it is indeed potentially disclosive. After the release of such data, each of the individuals in the equivalence class is seen as having a 50% probability of being positive in the listed disease, while before the data release the probability of it being positive was only a 1%.

- *Similarity attack.* l-diversity seeks to guarantee that each equivalence class contains different values and, depending on the instantiation, that none of these values dominates in terms of frequency of appearance. However, none of the previous properties of the equivalence classes provides meaningful disclosure risk limitation guarantees in presence of different but semantically close values of the sensitive attribute.

To deal with the above two issues, *t*-closeness proposes to use a relative measure for the variability of the values in the sensitive attribute, rather than an absolute measure that lacks semantic meaning. To that end, *t*-closeness seeks to limit the information gain of an observer from having access to the released data.

It is assumed that, before the data release, the observer has some prior knowledge about the distribution of the confidential attribute in the overall data set. Let us call P this prior distribution. Usually P is taken to be the marginal distribution of the sensitive attribute in the overall data set. The use of such prior knowledge can be justified by observing that, because the marginal distribution is not related to any specific individual, releasing it should be safe. Of course, when one of the individuals in the data set is known to have a distinctive value (e.g., in a given economic sector the largest firm in the sector could be easily identifiable by the value of the sensitive attribute) the release of the marginal distribution is indeed disclosive. In such case, a pre-processing step is needed on the confidential attribute, for instance, using top- or bottom-coding.

After the data release, the beliefs of the observer regarding the value of the confidential attribute of a specific individual change from P (the marginal distribution of the sensitive attribute) to Q (the distribution of the sensitive attribute in the corresponding equivalence class).

To limit the information gain that the observer obtains from having access to the released data, *t*-closeness limits the distance between between P and Q. Intuitively, when P and Q are equal, the released data do not reveal additional information about the sensitive attribute of any individual. The closer P and Q are, the less information the released data set provides about specific individuals.

Definition 6.2 *t*-Closeness [50]   An equivalence class is said to satisfy *t*-closeness if the distance between the distribution of a sensitive attribute in this class and the distribution of the attribute in the whole data set is no more than a threshold t. A data set is said to satisfy *t*-closeness if every equivalence class in it satisfies *t*-closeness.

The earth mover's distance

The definition of *t*-closeness does not prescribe any specific distance between distributions. Yet the earth mover's distance (EMD)[78] is the usual distance employed in *t*-closeness. The main advantage of EMD is that it is able to capture the semantic distance between values. $EMD(P, Q)$ measures the cost of transforming distribution P into distribution Q by moving probability mass. EMD is computed as the minimum transportation cost from the bins of P to the bins of Q, so it depends on how much mass is moved and how far it is moved (this can be a function of the semantic distance between values).

The EMD distance

   Consider a set of values $\{v_1, \ldots, v_r\}$ and two probability distributions $P = (p_1, \ldots, p_r)$ and $Q = (q_1, \ldots, q_r)$, where p_i and q_i are, respectively, the probabilities that

P and Q assign to v_i. Then $EMD(P, Q)$ is computed as the minimum transportation cost from the bins of P to the bins of Q, so it depends on how much mass is moved and how far it is moved. If we denote by d_{ij} the distance between values v_i and v_j and by f_{ij} the mass moved between v_i and v_j, $EMD(P, Q)$ can be computed as:

$$EMD(P, Q) = \min_{f_{ij}} \sum_{i=1}^{r} \sum_{j=1}^{r} d_{ij} f_{ij}$$

subject to:

$$f_{ij} \geq 0 \qquad\qquad 1 \leq i, j \leq r$$
$$p_i - \sum_{j=1}^{r} f_{ij} + \sum_{j=1}^{r} f_{ji} = q_i \qquad 1 \leq i \leq m$$
$$\sum_{i=1}^{m} \sum_{j=1}^{m} f_{ij} = \sum_{i=1}^{m} p_i = \sum_{i=1}^{m} q_i = 1.$$

Lemma 6.3   If $0 \leq d_{ij} \leq 1$ for all i, j then $0 \leq EMD(P, Q) \leq 1$.

Lemma 6.4   Let E_1 and E_2 be two equivalence classes. Let Q_1 and Q_2 be the distribution of the sensitive attribute in E_1 and E_2, respectively. Then

$$EMD(P, Q) \leq \frac{|E_1|}{|E_1| + |E_2|} EMD(P, Q_1) + \frac{|E_2|}{|E_1| + |E_2|} EMD(P, Q_2).$$

Computing EMD for numerical attributes. The first step in computing EMD is to define how the ground distance is measured. For a numerical attribute, the natural order can be used to measure such distance.

Definition 6.5   Ordered distance   Let $\{v_1, \ldots, v_r\}$ be set of values. The ordered distance is

$$ordered\_distance(v_i, v_j) = \frac{|rank(v_i) - rank(v_j)|}{r - 1}.$$

Let $P = (p_1, \ldots, p_r)$ and $Q = (q_1, \ldots, q_r)$ be probability distributions over $\{v_1, \ldots, v_r\}$. The EMD between P and Q can be computed as

$$EMD(P, Q) = \frac{1}{r - 1} \sum_{i=1}^{r} \left| \sum_{j=1}^{i} (p_i - q_i) \right|.$$

Computing EMD for categorical attributes. While for a numerical attribute there was a clear ground distance, for categorical attributes several distances are proposed according to the type of categorical attribute under consideration. Ordinal categorical attributes can be treated as numerical attributes. The ground distance is computed using the *ordered_distance* and the $EMD(P, Q)$ is computed according to the previous formula. For nominal categorical attributes, there is no relation between attribute values. In this case it is better to set the ground distance between any two different values of the attribute equal to 1. If $P = (p_1, \ldots, p_r)$ and $Q = (q_1, \ldots, q_r)$ are probability distributions over the values of the nominal categorical attribute, then *EMD* is computed as

$$EMD(P, Q) = \frac{1}{2} \sum_{i=1}^{r} |p_i - q_i|.$$

For hierarchical nominal attributes, the hierarchical relation between attribute values can be used to compute the ground distance. See [50] for more details on the computation of EMD on these types of categorical attributes and [97] for a specific application.

Generalization-based t-closeness

The general approach to attain t-closeness is to modify the algorithm used to satisfy k-anonymity so that the additional constraints of t-closeness are taken into account.

For t-closeness with EMD, the following properties guarantee that the Incognito algorithm for k-anonymity can be adapted to attain t-closeness.

Lemma 6.6   Generalization Property   Let X be a data set. Let Y be a generalization of X that satisfies t-closeness. If Z is a further generalization of Y, then Z satisfies t-closeness (with respect to X).

Lemma 6.7   Subset Property   Let X be a data set. Let Y be a data set satisfying t-closeness with respect to X. If Z is a data set obtained from Y by removing some attributes, then Z also satisfies t-closeness with respect to X.

6.3   SUMMARY

This chapter has introduced the l-diversity and t-closeness privacy models. These are refinements of the k-anonymity privacy model that seek to offer guarantees against attribute disclosure. l-diversity requires each of the equivalence classes to have diverse enough values for the confidential attribute. However, we have seen that l-diversity still has some problems. For instance, when the data are too skewed or when there are different values of the confidential attribute with similar meaning, l-diversity may not offer enough protection against attribute disclosure. t-closeness seeks to address such issues by introducing a relative measure of attribute disclosure risk: the distribution of the confidential attribute within each equivalence class should be similar to the distribution of the confidential attribute in the overall data set. In the next chapter, we detail how t-closeness can be enforced with k-anonymous microaggregation.

CHAPTER 7

t-Closeness Through Microaggregation

Similar to k-anonymity, the commonest way to attain t-closeness is to use generalization and suppression. In fact, the algorithms for k-anonymity based on those principles can be adapted to yield t-closeness by adding the t-closeness constraint in the search for a feasible minimal generalization: in [50] the Incognito algorithm and in [51] the Mondrian algorithm are respectively adapted to t-closeness.

On the other hand, as discussed in Section 5.4, microaggregation is a natural alternative to attain k-anonymity that offers several advantages over generalization and suppression (mostly related to a better preservation of data utility). When using microaggregation for t-closeness, one has the additional constraint that the distance between the distribution of the confidential attribute within each of the clusters generated by microaggregation and the distribution in the entire data set must be less than t. This makes reaching t-closeness more complex, because we have to reconcile the possibly conflicting goals of maximizing the within-cluster homogeneity of the quasi-identifiers and fulfilling the condition on the distance between the distributions of the confidential attributes. Nevertheless, one can expect significant utility gains w.r.t. generalization and suppression [98].

In the sequel, three different algorithms to trade off these conflicting goals are detailed [98]. The first algorithm is based on performing microaggregation in the usual way, and then merging clusters as much as needed to satisfy the t-closeness condition. This first algorithm is simple and it can be combined with any microaggregation algorithm, yet it may perform poorly regarding utility because clusters may end up being quite large. The other algorithms modify the microaggregation algorithm for it to take t-closeness into account, in an attempt to improve the utility of the anonymized data set. Two variants are proposed: k-anonymity-first (which generates each cluster based on the quasi-identifiers and then refines it to satisfy t-closeness) and t-closeness-first (which generates each cluster based on both quasi-identifier attributes and confidential attributes, so that it satisfies t-closeness by design from the very beginning).

7.1 STANDARD MICROAGGREGATION AND MERGING

Generating a t-close data set via generalization is essentially an optimization problem: one must find a minimal generalization that satisfies t-closeness. A common way to find a solution is to iteratively generalize one of the attributes (selected according to some quality criterion) until the resulting data set satisfies *t*-closeness. The first method to attain *t*-closeness via microaggregation follows a similar approach. We microaggregate and then merge clusters of records in the microaggregated data set; we use the distance between the quasi-identifiers of the microaggregated clusters as the quality criterion to select which groups are to be merged (in order to minimize the information loss of the microaggregation).

Initially, the microaggregation algorithm is run on the quasi-identifier attributes of the original data set; this step produces a *k*-anonymous data set. Then, clusters of microaggregated records are merged until *t*-closeness is satisfied (with EMD as a distance, see Section 6.2). We iteratively improve the level of *t*-closeness by: i) selecting the cluster whose confidential attribute distribution is most different from the confidential attribute distribution in the entire data set (that is, the cluster farthest from satisfying *t*-closeness); and ii) merging it with the cluster closest to it in terms of quasi-identifiers. See Algorithm 4.

Algorithm 4 *t*-closeness through microaggregation and merging of microaggregated groups of records

---

Data: X: original data set

      k: minimum cluster size

      t: t-closeness level

Result: Set of clusters satisfying k-anonymity and t-closeness

X'=microaggregation(X, k)

while $EMD(X', X) > t$ **do**

    C = cluster in X' with the greatest EMD to X

    C' = cluster in X' closest to C in terms of QIs

    X' = merge C and C' in X'

end while

return X'

Note that Algorithm 4 always returns a *t*-close data set. In the worst case, all clusters are eventually merged into a single one and EMD becomes zero. The computational cost of Algorithm 4 is the sum of the cost of the initial microaggregation and the cost of merging clusters. Although optimal multivariate microaggregation is NP-hard, several heuristic approximations exist with quadratic cost on the number n of records of X (e.g., MDAV [26], V-MDAV [88]). For the merging part, the fact that computing EMD for numerical data has linear cost turns the merging quadratic. More precisely, the cost of Algorithm 4 is $\max\{\mathcal{O}(microaggregation), n^2/k\}$. If MDAV is used for microaggregation, the cost is $\mathcal{O}(n^2/k)$.

7.2 t-CLOSENESS AWARE MICROAGGREGATION: k-ANONYMITY-FIRST

Algorithm 4 consists of two clearly defined steps: first microaggregate and then merge clusters until t-closeness is satisfied. In the microaggregation step any standard microaggregation algorithm can be used because the enforcement of t-closeness takes place only after microaggregation is complete. As a result, the algorithm is quite clear, but the utility of the anonymized data set may be far from optimal. If, instead of deferring the enforcement of t-closeness to the second step, we make the microaggregation algorithm aware of the t-closeness constraints at the time of cluster formation, the size of the resulting clusters and also information loss can be expected to be smaller.

Algorithm 5 microaggregates according to the above idea. It initially generates a cluster of size k based on the quasi-identifier attributes. Then the cluster is iteratively refined until t-closeness is satisfied. In the refinement, the algorithm checks whether t-closeness is satisfied and, if it is not, it selects the closest record not in the cluster based on the quasi-identifiers and swaps it with a record in the cluster selected so that the EMD to the distribution of the entire data set is minimized. Instead of replacing the records already added to a cluster, we could have opted for adding additional records until t-closeness is satisfied. This latter approach was discarded because it led to large clusters when the dependence between quasi-identifiers and confidential attributes is high. In this case, clusters homogeneous in terms of quasi-identifiers tend to be homogeneous in terms of confidential attributes, so the within-cluster distribution of the confidential attribute differs from its distribution in the entire data set unless the cluster is (nearly) as big as the entire data set.

It may happen that the records in the data set are exhausted before t-closeness is satisfied. This is most likely when the number of remaining unclustered records is small (for instance, when the last cluster is formed). Thus, Algorithm 5 alone cannot guarantee that t-closeness is satisfied. A way to circumvent this shortcoming is to use Algorithm 5 as the microaggregation function in Algorithm 4. By taking into account t-closeness at the time of cluster formation (as Algorithm 5 does), the number of cluster mergers in Algorithm 4 can be expected to be small and, therefore, the utility of the resulting anonymized data set can be expected to be reasonably good. Algorithm 5 makes an intensive use of the EMD distance. Due to this and to the cost of computing EMD, Algorithm 5 may be rather slow. More precisely, it has order $\mathcal{O}(n^3/k)$ in the worst case, and order $\mathcal{O}(n^2/k)$ in the best case (when no record swaps are required).

7.3 t-CLOSENESS AWARE MICROAGGREGATION: t-CLOSENESS-FIRST

Algorithm 5 modified the microaggregation for it to build the clusters in a t-closeness aware manner. The clustering algorithm, however, kept the focus on the quasi-identifiers (records were selected based on the quasi-identifiers) and did not guarantee that every cluster satisfies t-closeness.

Algorithm 5 k-Anonymity-first t-closeness aware microaggregation algorithm *(Continues.)*

Function k-Anonymity-first

       Data: X: original data set

              k: minimum cluster size

              t: t-closeness level

       Result Set of clusters satisfying k-anonymity and t-closeness $Clusters = \emptyset$

       $X' = X$

       while $X' \neq \emptyset$

              x_a = average record of X'

              x_0 = most distant record from x_a in X'

              C = GenerateCluster(x_0, X', X, k, t)

              $X' = X' \setminus C$

              $Clusters = Clusters \cup \{C\}$

              if $X' \neq \emptyset$

                     x_1 = most distant record from x_0 in X'

                     C = GenerateCluster(x_1, X', X, k, t)

                     $X' = X' \setminus C$

                     $Clusters = Clusters \cup \{C\}$

              end if

       end while

       return *Clusters*

end function

Moreover, it could be computationally costly for large data sets. The algorithm proposed in this section prioritizes the confidential attribute, thereby making it possible to guarantee that all clusters satisfy t-closeness. We assume in this section that the values of the confidential attribute(s) can be ranked, that is, be ordered in some way. For numerical or categorical ordinal attributes, ranking is straightforward. Even for categorical nominal attributes, the ranking assumption is less restrictive than it appears, because the same distance metrics that are used to microaggregate these types of attributes can be used to rank them (e.g., the marginality distance in [23, 97] and other semantic distances applied to data microaggregation in [8, 57]). We start by evaluating some of the properties of the EMD distance with respect to microaggregation. To minimize EMD between the distributions of the confidential attribute within a cluster and in the entire data set, the values of the confidential attribute in the cluster must be as spread as possible over the entire data

---

Algorithm 5 *(Continued.)* k-Anonymity-first t-closeness aware microaggregation algorithm

---

Function GenerateCluster(x, X', X, k, t)

  Data: x: source record for the cluster

         X': remaining unclustered records of X

         X: original data set

         k: minimum cluster size

         t: desired t-closeness level

  Result t-close cluster of k (or more) records

  if $|X'| < 2k$

      $C = X'$

  else

      $C = k$ closest records to x in X' (including x itself)

      $X' = X' \setminus C$

      while $EMD(C, X) > t$ and $X' \neq \emptyset$

          y = record in X' that is closest to x

          y' = record C that minimizes $EMD(C \cup \{y\} \setminus \{y'\}, X)$

          if $EMD(C \cup \{y\} \setminus \{y'\}, X) < EMD(C, X)$

              $C = C \cup \{y\} \setminus \{y'\}$

          end if

          $X' = X' \setminus \{y\}$

      end while

  end if

  return C

End Function

---

set. Consider the case of a cluster with k records. The following proposition lower-bounds EMD for such a cluster.

Proposition 7.1   Let X be a data set with n records, A be a confidential attribute of X whose values can be ranked, and C be a cluster of size k. The earth mover's distance between C and X with respect to attribute A satisfies:

$$EMD_A(C, X) \geq \frac{(n + k)(n - k)}{4n(n - 1)k}.$$

If k divides n, this lower bound is tight.

Proof. EMD can intuitively be seen as the amount of work needed to transform the distribution of attribute A within C into the distribution of A over X. The "amount of work" includes two factors: (i) the amount of probability mass that needs to be moved and (ii) the distance of the movement.

When computing EMD for t-closeness, the distance of the movements of probability mass for numerical attributes is measured as the ordered distance, that is, the difference between the ranks of the values of A in X divided by $n-1$.

For the sake of simplicity, assume that k divides n. If that is not the case, the distance will be slightly greater, so the lower bound we compute is still valid. The probability mass of each of the values of A is constant and equal to $1/n$ in X, and it is constant and equal to $1/k$ in C. This means that the first factor that determines the EMD (the amount of probability mass to be moved) is fixed. Therefore, to minimize EMD we must minimize the second factor (the distance by which the probability mass must be moved). Clearly, to minimize the distance, the i-th value of A in the cluster must lie in the middle of the i-th group of n/k records of X. Figure 7.1 illustrates this fact.

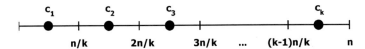

Figure 7.1: t-closeness first, case k divides n. Confidential attribute values $\{c_1, c_2, \ldots, c_k\}$ of the cluster C that minimizes the earth mover's distance to X. When the confidential attribute values in X are grouped in k subsets of n/k values, c_i is the median of the i-th subset for $i = 1, \ldots, k$.

In Figure 7.1 and using the ordered distance, the earth mover's distance can be computed as k times the cost of distributing the probability mass of element c_1 among the n/k elements in the first subset:

$$\min(EMD) = k \times \sum_{t=1}^{n/k} \frac{1}{n} \frac{|i - \lfloor n/k + 1/2 \rfloor|}{n - 1} = \frac{(n+k)(n-k)}{4n(n-1)k}. \tag{7.1}$$

Formula (7.1) takes element $(n/k + 1)/2$ as the middle element of a cluster with n/k elements. Strictly speaking, this is only possible when n/k is odd. When n/k is even, we ought to take either $\lfloor (n/k + 1)/2 \rfloor$, the element just before the middle, or $\lceil (n/k + 1)/2 \rceil$, the element just after the middle. In any case, the EMD ends up being the same as the one obtained in Formula (7.1). $\qquad\square$

Note that, once n and t are fixed, Proposition 7.1 determines the minimum value of k required for EMD to be smaller than t. An issue with the construction of the k values $c_1, \ldots, c_k$ depicted in Figure 7.1 is that it is too restrictive. For instance, for given values of n and t, if the minimal EMD value computed in Proposition 7.1 is exactly equal to t, then only clusters having as confidential attribute values $c_1, \ldots, c_k$ satisfy t-closeness (there may be only one such cluster). Any other cluster having different confidential attribute values does not satisfy t-closeness. Moreover, in the construction of Figure 7.1, the clusters are generated based only on the values of the confidential attribute, which may lead to a large information loss in terms of the quasi-identifiers.

Given the limitations pointed out above, our goal is to guarantee that the EMD of the clusters is below a specific value but allowing the clustering algorithm enough freedom to select appropriate records (in terms of quasi-identifiers) for each of the clusters. The approach that we propose is similar to the one of Figure 7.1: we group the records in X into k subsets based on the confidential attribute and we then generate clusters based on the quasi-identifiers with the constraint that each cluster should contain one record from each of the k subsets (the specific record is selected based on the quasi-identifier attributes). Proposition 7.2 gives an upper bound on the level of t-closeness that we attain. To simplify the derivation and the proof, we assume in the proposition that k divides n.

Proposition 7.2   Let X be a data set with n records and let A be a confidential attribute of X whose values can be ranked. Let $S = \{S_1, \ldots, S_k\}$ be a partition of the records in X into k subsets of n/k records in ascending order of the attribute A. Let C be a cluster that contains exactly one record from each of the subsets S_i, for $i = 1, \ldots, k$. Then

$$EMD(C, X) \leq \frac{n - k}{2(n - 1)k}.$$

Proof. The factors that determine EMD are: (i) the amount of probability mass that needs to be moved and (ii) the distance by which it is moved. The first factor is fixed and cannot be modified: each of the records in X has probability mass $1/n$, and each of the records in C has probability mass of $1/k$. As to the second factor, to find an upper bound to EMD, we need to consider a cluster C that maximizes EMD: the records selected for inclusion into C must be at the lower (or upper) end of the sets S_i for $i = 1, \ldots, k$. This is depicted in Figure 7.2. (Note the analogy with the proof of Proposition 7.1: there we took the median of each S_i to minimize EMD.)

Figure 7.2:   *t*-closeness first, case k divides n. Confidential attribute values $\{c_1, c_2, \ldots, c_k\}$ of the cluster C that maximizes the earth mover's distance to X. When the confidential attribute values in X are grouped in k subsets of n/k values, c_i is taken as the minimum value of the i-th subset for $i = 1, \ldots, k$.

EMD for the case in Figure 7.2 can be computed as k times the cost of distributing the probability mass of c_1 among the n/k elements of S_1:

$$\max(EMD) = k \times \sum_{i=1}^{n/k} \frac{1}{n} \frac{i - 1}{n - 1} = \frac{n - k}{2(n - 1)k}. \tag{7.2}$$

□

With the upper bound on EMD given by Proposition 7.2, we can determine the cluster size required in the microaggregation: just replace $EMD(C, X)$ by t on the left-hand side of the bound and solve for k to get a lower bound for k. For a data set containing n records and for a required level of t-closeness and k-anonymity, the cluster size must be

$$\max\left\{k, \left\lceil \frac{n}{2(n-1)t+1} \right\rceil \right\}. \tag{7.3}$$

To keep things simple, so far we have assumed that k divides n. However, the algorithm to generate t-close data sets must work even if that is not the case. If discarding some records from the original data set is a viable option, we could discard records until k divides the new n, and proceed as described above. If records cannot be discarded, some of the clusters would need to contain more than k records. In particular, we may allow some clusters to have either k or $k + 1$ records.

If we group the records into k sets with $\lfloor n/k \rfloor$ records, then $r = n \mod k$ records remain. We propose to assign the remaining r records to one of the subsets. Then, when generating the clusters, two records from this subset are added to the first r clusters. This is only possible if $r \le \lfloor n/k \rfloor$ (the number of remaining records is not greater than the number of generated clusters); otherwise, there will be records not assigned to any cluster. Note, however, that using a cluster size k with $r \ge \lfloor n/k \rfloor$ makes no sense: since all clusters receive more than k records, what is reasonable is to adapt to reality by increasing k. Specifically, to avoid having $r \ge \lfloor n/k \rfloor$, k is adjusted as

$$k = k + \lfloor (n \mod k)/\lfloor n/k \rfloor \rfloor. \tag{7.4}$$

Adding two records from one of the subsets to a cluster increases the EMD of the cluster. To minimize the impact over the EMD, we need to reduce the work required to distribute the probability mass of the extra record across the whole range of values. Hence, the extra record must be close to the median record of the data set. Figure 7.3 illustrates the types of clusters that we allow when k is odd (there is a single subset in the middle), and Figure 7.4 illustrates the types of clusters that we allow when k is even (there are two subsets in the middle). Essentially, when k is odd, the additional records are added to $S_{(k+1)/2}$ (the subset in the middle); then, we generate clusters with size k and clusters with size $k + 1$, which take two records from $S_{(k+1)/2}$. When k is even, the additional records are split between $S_{(k-1)/2}$ and $S_{(k+1)/2}$ (the subsets in the middle); then, we generate clusters with size k and clusters with size $k + 1$, some with an additional record from $S_{(k-1)/2}$ and some from $S_{k/2}$.

Just as we did in Proposition 7.2, we can compute an upper bound for the EMD of the clusters depicted in Figures 7.3 and 7.4. The EMD of a cluster C measures the cost of transforming the distribution of C into the distribution of the entire data set. The cost of the probability redistribution can be computed in two steps as follows. First, we want the weight of each subset $S_1, \ldots, S_k$ in cluster C (the proportion of records in C coming from each subset) to be equal to the weight of the subset in the data set; to this end, we redistribute the probability mass of the

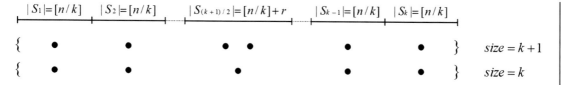

Figure 7.3: t-closeness first, case k does not divide n. Types of clusters when k is odd. Top row, the data set is split into k subsets. Central row, cluster with $k + 1$ records. Bottom row, cluster with k records.

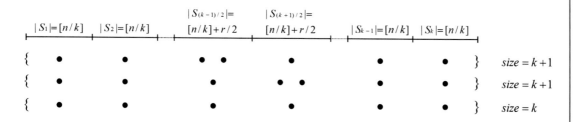

Figure 7.4: t-closeness first, case k does not divide n. Types of clusters when k is even. Top row, the data set is split into k subsets. Central rows, clusters with $k + 1$ records (one with two records from $S_{(k-1)/2}$ and the other with two records from $S_{(k+1)/2}$). Bottom row, cluster with k records.

cluster between subsets. This redistribution cost, $cost_0$, equals the EMD between the cluster and the data set when the distributions have been discretized to the subsets. Then, for each subset $S_i \in \{S_1, \ldots, S_k\}$, we compute $cost_i$, an upper bound of the cost of distributing the probability mass $|S_i|/n$ assigned to the subset among its elements (this is analogous to the mass distribution in the proof of Proposition 7.2). The EMD is the sum $cost_0 + cost_1 + \ldots + cost_k$. The fact that there are subsets with different sizes and there are clusters with different sizes makes formulas quite tedious and unwieldy, even though the resulting bounds on EMD are very similar to the one obtained in Proposition 7.2. For these reasons, we will use the latter as an approximation even when k does not divide n; in particular, we will determine the cluster size using Expression (7.3).

Algorithm 6 formalizes the above described procedure to generate a k-anonymous t-close data set. It makes use of Expressions (7.3) and (7.4) to determine and adjust the cluster size, respectively.

In terms of computational cost, Algorithm 6 has a great advantage over Algorithms 4 and 5: when running Algorithm 6, we know that by construction the generated clusters satisfy t-closeness, so there is no need to compute any EMD distance. Algorithm 6 has cost $\mathcal{O}(n^2/k)$, the same cost order as MDAV (on which it is based). Actually, Algorithm 6 is even slightly more efficient than MDAV: all operations being equal, some of the computations MDAV performs on the entire data set are performed by Algorithm 6 just on one of the subsets of n/k records.

Algorithm 6 t-closeness-first microaggregation algorithm. Distances between records are computed in terms of the quasi-identifiers *(Continues.)*

Data: X: original data set

$\quad\quad$ n: size of X

$\quad\quad$ k: minimum cluster size

$\quad\quad$ t: t-closeness level

Result Set of clusters satisfying k-anonymity and t-closeness $k = \max\{k, \lceil \frac{n}{2(n-1)t+1} \rceil\}$

$k = k + \lceil (n \bmod k)/\lfloor n/k \rfloor \rceil$

Clusters $= \emptyset$

Split X into $S_1, \ldots, S_k$ subsets with $\lfloor n/k \rfloor$ records in ascending order of the confidential attribute, with any remaining $(n \bmod k)$ records assigned to the central subset(s)

while $X \neq \emptyset$

$\quad\quad$ x_a = average record of X

$\quad\quad$ x_0 = most distant record from x_a in X

$\quad\quad$ $C = \emptyset$

$\quad\quad$ **for** $i = 1, \ldots, k$

$\quad\quad\quad\quad$ x = closest record to x_0 in S_i

$\quad\quad\quad\quad$ $C = C \cup \{x\}$

$\quad\quad\quad\quad$ $S_i = S_i \setminus \{x\}$

$\quad\quad\quad\quad$ $X = X \setminus \{x\}$

$\quad\quad\quad\quad$ *// Take second record from S_i if it contains extra records and no extra record*

$\quad\quad\quad\quad$ *// has been already added to C*

$\quad\quad\quad\quad$ **if** $|S_i| > |S_1|$ **and** $|C| = i$

$\quad\quad\quad\quad\quad\quad$ x = closest record to x_0 in S_i

$\quad\quad\quad\quad\quad\quad$ $C = C \cup \{x\}$

$\quad\quad\quad\quad\quad\quad$ $S_i = S_i \setminus \{x\}$

$\quad\quad\quad\quad\quad\quad$ $X = X \setminus \{x\}$

$\quad\quad\quad\quad$ **end if**

$\quad\quad$ **end for**

7.4   SUMMARY

This chapter has detailed three microaggregation-based methods to attain k-anonymous t-closeness, which offer several *a priori* benefits over generalization/recoding and local suppression. The first one is a simple merging step that can be run after any microaggregation algorithm. The other two algorithms, k-anonymity-first and t-closeness-first, take the t-closeness requirement into account at the moment of cluster formation during microaggregation. The t-closeness-first algorithm considers t-closeness earliest and provides the best results: smallest average cluster size, smallest SSE for a given level of t-closeness, and shortest run time (because the actual microag-

Algorithm 6 *(Continued.)* t-closeness-first microaggregation algorithm. Distances between records are computed in terms of the quasi-identifiers

> $Clusters = Clusters \cup \{C\}$
> **if** $X \neq \emptyset$
> > x_1 = most distant record from x_0 in X
> > $C = \emptyset$
> > **for** $i = 1, \ldots, k$
> > > x = closest record to x_1 in S_i
> > > $C = C \cup \{x\}$
> > > $S_i = S_i \setminus \{x\}$
> > > $X = X \setminus \{x\}$
> > > **if** $|S_i| > |S_1|$ **and** $|C| = i$
> > > > x = closest record to x_1 in S_i
> > > > $C = C \cup \{x\}$
> > > > $S_i = S_i \setminus \{x\}$
> > > > $X = X \setminus \{x\}$
> > > **end if**
> > **end for**
> > $Clusters = Clusters \cup \{C\}$
> **end if**
> **end while**
> **return** *Clusters*

gregation level is computed beforehand according to the values of k and t). Thus, considering the t-closeness requirement from the very beginning turns out to be the best option.

CHAPTER 8

Differential Privacy

Differential privacy is a privacy model that has become quite popular because of the strong privacy guarantees it provides. Differential privacy was initially stated as a privacy guarantee in an interactive setting, where queries are submitted to a database containing the original individual records. However, it is general enough to deal with microdata releases. The principle underlying differential privacy is that the presence or absence of any single individual record in the database or data set should be unnoticeable when looking at the responses returned for the queries.

8.1 DEFINITION

Differential privacy was originally proposed in [29] as a privacy model in the interactive setting, that is, to protect the outcomes of queries to a database. The assumption is that an anonymization mechanism sits between the user submitting queries and the database answering them. To preserve the privacy of individuals, the knowledge gain derived from the presence of an individual in the data set must be limited.

Definition 8.1 (ϵ, δ)-**differential privacy** A randomized function κ gives (ϵ, δ)-differential privacy if, for all data sets X_1 and X_2 that differ in one record, and all $S \subset Range(\kappa)$, we have

$$\Pr(\kappa(X_1) \in S) \leq \exp(\epsilon) \times \Pr(\kappa(X_2) \in S) + \delta.$$

We will use the notation ϵ-differential privacy to denote $(\epsilon, 0)$-differential privacy.

Let $\mathcal{D}$ be the domain of possible data sets. When faced with the query f, the goal in differential privacy is to come up with a differentially private mechanism, κ_f, that approximates f as closely as possible and returns the response given by κ_f.

The computational mechanism to attain differential privacy is often called a differentially private sanitizer. Sanitizers can rely on addition of noise (Laplace distributed, geometrically distributed, or using the optimal distribution) calibrated to the global sensitivity, addition of noise calibrated to the smooth sensitivity, or the exponential mechanism.

A good property of differential privacy (not offered by previous privacy models such as k-anonymity, l-diversity, or t-closeness) is that the combination of several differentially private results still satisfies differential privacy, although with different parameters. The following composition theorems describe several types of composition.

Theorem 8.2   Sequential composition   Let κ_1 be a randomized function giving (ϵ_1, δ_1)-differential privacy, and let κ_2 be a randomized function giving (ϵ_2, δ_2)-differential privacy. Any deterministic function of (κ_1, κ_2) gives $(\epsilon_1 + \epsilon_2, \delta_1 \delta_2)$-differential privacy.

When differentially private mechanisms are applied to disjoint subsets of records, the level of differential privacy of the original mechanism is preserved.

Theorem 8.3   Parallel composition   Let κ_1 and κ_2 be randomized functions giving (ϵ, δ)-differential privacy. If the mechanism κ_1 and κ_2 are computed over disjoint subsets of records, then any deterministic function of (κ_1, κ_2) gives (ϵ, δ)-differential privacy.

Another composition theorem known as advanced composition is presented in [30].

8.2   CALIBRATION TO THE GLOBAL SENSITIVITY

Let $\mathcal{D}$ be the domain of possible data sets. Let $f : \mathcal{D} \to \mathbb{R}^k$ be a query function that maps data sets to vectors of real numbers. Here we seek to come up with a differentially private mechanism κ_f of the form $\kappa_f(X) = f(X) + Noise$, where the distribution of the random noise is independent of the actual data set X.

The amount of noise required depends on the variability of the function f between neighbor data sets (data sets that differ in one record). The greater the l_1-sensitivity, the greater the amount of noise that will be required to mask the effect of any single individual record in the response of the query.

Definition 8.4 l_1-sensitivity   The l_1-sensitivity of a function $f : \mathcal{D} \to \mathbb{R}^k$ is

$$\Delta f = \max_{\substack{x, y \in \mathcal{D} \\ d(x, y) = 1}} \| f(x) - f(y) \|_1 .$$

The Laplace mechanism
Random noise with Laplace distribution is commonly used to attain ϵ-differential privacy. The density of the Laplace distribution with mean μ and scale b, $Lap(\mu, b)$, is

$$Lap_{\mu, b}(x) = \frac{1}{2b} \exp\left(-\frac{|x|}{b}\right).$$

Theorem 8.5 The Laplace mechanism   Let $f : \mathcal{D} \to \mathbb{R}^k$ be a function mapping data sets to vectors of real numbers. The Laplace mechanism

$$\mathcal{M}_L(x, f, \epsilon) = f(x) + (N_1, \ldots, N_k)$$

where $N_i \sim Lap(0, \Delta f/\epsilon)$ are independent random variables, gives ϵ-differential privacy.

The optimal a.c. mechanism

The Laplace mechanism is the most common choice to obtain ϵ-differential privacy for a given query $f : \mathcal{D} \to \mathbb{R}^k$. However, Laplace noise is not optimal, in the sense that other noise distributions can yield ϵ-differential privacy while having their probability mass more concentrated around zero.

Deciding which one among a pair of random noise distributions, N_1 and N_2, yields greater utility is a question that may depend on the users' preferences. The goal here is to come up with an optimality notion that is independent from the users' preferences. If N_1 can be constructed from N_2 by moving some of the probability mass toward zero (but without going beyond zero), then N_1 must always be preferred to N_2. The reason is that the probability mass of N_1 is more concentrated around zero, and thus the distortion introduced by N_1 is smaller. A rational user always prefers less distortion and, therefore, prefers N_1 to N_2.

For a random noise distribution in $\mathbb{R}$, we use the notation $< 0, \alpha >$, where $\alpha \in \mathbb{R}$, to denote the interval $[0, \alpha]$ when $\alpha \geq 0$, and the interval $[\alpha, 0]$ when $\alpha \leq 0$. If N_1 can be constructed from N_2 by moving some of the probability mass toward zero, it must be $\Pr(N_1 \in < 0, \alpha >) \geq \Pr(N_2 \in < 0, \alpha >)$ for any $\alpha \in \mathbb{R}$. Thus we define:

Definition 8.6   Let N_1 and N_2 be two random distributions on $\mathbb{R}$. We say that N_1 is smaller than N_2, denoted by $N_1 \leq N_2$ if $\Pr(N_1 \in < 0, \alpha >) \geq \Pr(N_2 \in < 0, \alpha >)$ for any $\alpha \in \mathbb{R}$. We say that N_1 is strictly smaller than N_2, denoted by $N_1 < N_2$, if some of the previous inequalities are strict.

The previous definition deals only with univariate noise distributions. The concept of optimal multivariate noise can also be defined. However, dealing with multiple dimensions makes things more complex. Here we restrict the discussion to univariate random noises. See [92] for more details on the multivariate case.

We use the previous order relationship to define the concept of optimal random noise. A noise is optimal within a class if there is no other noise in the class that is strictly smaller.

Definition 8.7   A random noise distribution N_1 is optimal within a class $\mathcal{C}$ of random noise distributions if N_1 is minimal within $\mathcal{C}$; in other words, there is no other random noise $N_2 \in \mathcal{C}$ such that $N_2 < N_1$.

The concept of optimality is relative to a specific class $\mathcal{C}$ of random noise distributions. The goal is to determine the optimal noise for a query function f that take values in $\mathbb{R}$. To this end, we first need to determine which is the class of random noises $\mathcal{C}$ that provide differential privacy for f. Indeed, $\mathcal{C}$ can be directly defined as the class of noise distributions that satisfy the requirements of differential privacy. However, such definition is not very useful in the construction of the optimal noise. Here we seek to characterize the noise distributions that give ϵ-differential privacy in terms of the density function.

Proposition 8.8   Let N be an a.c. random noise with values in $\mathbb{R}$. Let f_N be the density function of N. For a query function $f : \mathcal{D} \to \mathbb{R}$, the mechanism $f + N$ gives ϵ-differential privacy if

$$f_N(x) \le \exp(\epsilon) \times f_N(x + \Delta f) \tag{8.1}$$

for all $x \in \mathbb{R}$ continuity point of f_N such that $x + \Delta f$ is also a continuity point.

Now we show that the Laplace distribution is not optimal. The basic idea is to concentrate the probability mass around 0 as much as possible. This can only be done to a certain extent, because Inequality (8.1) limits our capability to do so.

In the construction of the distribution we will split the domain of f_N into intervals of the form $[i\Delta f, (i + 1)\Delta f]$ where $i \in \mathbb{Z}$. For each interval we will redistribute the probability mass that f_N assigns to that interval. The new density function will take only two values (see Figure 8.1): $\max_{x \in [i\Delta f, (i+1)\Delta f]} f_N(x)$ at the portion of the interval closer to zero and $\min_{x \in [i\Delta f, (i+1)\Delta f]} f_N(x)$ at the portion of the interval farther from zero. The result is an absolutely continuous distribution where the probability mass has clearly been moved toward zero. It can be checked that this distribution satisfies Inequality (8.1).

The process used to show that the Laplace distribution is not optimal for ϵ-differential privacy can be generalized to show that the same construction is possible independently of the initial noise distribution N.

Theorem 8.9   Let N be an a.c. random noise with zero mean that provides ϵ-differential privacy to a query function f. Then there exists a random noise N' with density of the form

$$f_{N'}(x) = \begin{cases} M \exp(-i\epsilon) & x \in [-d - (i + 1)\Delta f, -d - i\Delta f], i \in \mathbb{N} \\ M & x \in [-d, 0] \\ M & x \in [0, d] \\ M \exp(-i\epsilon) & x \in [d + i\Delta f, d + (i + 1)\Delta f], i \in \mathbb{N} \end{cases}$$

that provides ϵ-differential privacy to f and satisfies $N' \le N$.

Now it only remains to show that the distributions constructed in Theorem 8.9 are indeed optimal. This is done by checking that, for such distributions, it is not possible to move the probability mass toward 0 any more. That is, if we try to move more probability mass toward 0, ϵ-differential privacy stops being satisfied.

Theorem 8.10   Let N be a random noise distribution with density function f_N of the form specified in Theorem 8.9. Then N is optimal at providing ϵ-differential privacy.

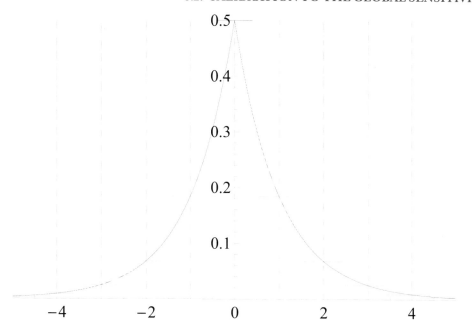

Figure 8.1: Construction of an optimal distribution based on the Laplace(0,1) distribution.

The discrete Laplace mechanism

The previous mechanisms (based on the addition of a random noise with values in $\mathbb{R}$) are capable of providing differential privacy to query functions with values in $\mathbb{Z}$. However, for such query functions, the use of a noise distribution with support over $\mathbb{Z}$ is a better option. The discrete version of the Laplace distribution is defined as:

Definition 8.11   Discrete Laplace distribution [46]   A random variable N follows the discrete Laplace distribution with parameter $\alpha \in (0, 1)$, denoted by $DL(\alpha)$, if for all $k \in \mathbb{Z}$

$$\Pr(N = i) = \frac{1 - \alpha}{1 + \alpha} \alpha^{|i|}.$$

Like the Laplace distribution, the discrete Laplace distribution can be used to attain ϵ-differential privacy. For this purpose, parameter α must be adjusted to the desired level of differential privacy and to the global sensitivity of the query.

Theorem 8.12   The discrete Laplace mechanism   Let $f : \mathcal{D} \to \mathbb{Z}^k$ be a function mapping data sets to vectors of integers. The discrete Laplace mechanism

$$\mathcal{M}_{DL}(x, f, \epsilon) = f(x) + (N_1, \ldots, N_k)$$

where $N_i \sim DL(\exp(-\epsilon / \Delta f))$ are independent random variables, gives ϵ-differential privacy.

8.3   CALIBRATION TO THE SMOOTH SENSITIVITY

The global sensitivity measures the greatest variability in the query function f between neighbor data sets. Being an upper bound on the variability, most of the times the variability of f between a specific data set X and its neighbors is usually lower than the global sensitivity. This is known as the local sensitivity.

Definition 8.13   Local sensitivity [68]   For $f : \mathcal{D} \to \mathbb{R}^k$ and $X \in \mathcal{D}$, the local sensitivity of f at X is

$$LS_f(X) = \max_{y:d(y,X)=1} \| f(X) - f(y) \|_1 .$$

The difference between local and global sensitivities can be large. This is illustrated in the following example for a function that returns the median of a list of values.

Example 8.14   Consider a data set $X = \{x_1, \ldots, x_n\}$ where each record corresponds to a value in $\{0, 1\}$. To make things simple we assume that the number of records is odd (so that the median corresponds to a single record): $n = 2m + 1$. The global sensitivity of the median is 1, since we can consider the neighbor data sets:

$$\{0, \overset{m}{\ldots}, 0, 1, \overset{m+1}{\ldots}, 1\} \to median = 0$$
$$\{0, \overset{m+1}{\ldots}, 0, 1, \overset{m}{\ldots}, 1\} \to median = 1.$$

The local sensitivity is, except for the two previous data sets, always 0. The reason is that, except for the previous data sets, changing the value of a record does not modify the median.

Releasing the value of a query with the addition of a noise whose magnitude is proportional to the local sensitivity (rather than the global sensitivity) would result in a significantly more accurate response. However, using the local sensitivity in the mechanisms designed for global sensitivity does not yield differential privacy.

Example 8.15   Consider the data sets: $\{0, \overset{m+2}{\ldots}, 0, 1, \overset{m-1}{\ldots}, 1\}$ and $\{0, \overset{m+1}{\ldots}, 0, 1, \overset{m}{\ldots}, 1\}$. In both cases the median is 0, but the local sensitivity differs: it is 0 in the first one and 1 in the second one.

	median	local sensitivity
$X = \{0, \overset{m+2}{\ldots}, 0, 1, \overset{m-1}{\ldots}, 1\}$	0	0
$X' = \{0, \overset{m+1}{\ldots}, 0, 1, \overset{m}{\ldots}, 1\}$	0	1

Given that the local sensitivity for X' is 0, adding a noise proportional to the local sensitivity does not modify the median; thus the probability of getting 1 is 0. For $(\epsilon, 0)$-differential privacy to be satisfied, the probability of getting 1 for X' must also be 0. However, that is not the case because the local sensitivity in this case is different from 0.

The previous example shows that the amount of noise used in a data set should not only be proportional to its local sensitivity but also take into account the local sensitivity of neighbor data sets. This is the smooth sensitivity.

Definition 8.16   Smooth sensitivity   For $\beta > 0$ the β-smooth sensitivity of f is

$$S_{f,\beta}(x) = \max_{y \in \mathcal{D}}(LS_f(y) \exp(-\beta d(x, y))).$$

The greater the β parameter, the smaller the dependence of the smooth sensitivity on the local sensitivity of neighbor data sets. Thus, the amount of noise required to attain (ϵ, δ)-differential privacy must depend on factors other than the smooth sensitivity. In particular we are interested in (α, β)-admissible noise distributions, which are distributions that bound the change in probability due to sliding and dilatation.

Definition 8.17   Admissible noise distribution   The distribution of a random noise N on $\mathbb{R}^k$ is (α, β)-admissible for (ϵ, δ)-differential privacy if for all $\|\Delta\| \leq \alpha$ and $|\lambda| \leq \beta$ and all $S \subset \mathbb{R}^k$ we have the sliding property

$$\Pr(N \in S) \leq \exp(\epsilon/2) \Pr(N \in S + \Delta) + \frac{\delta}{2}$$

and the dilatation property

$$\Pr(N \in S) \leq \exp(\epsilon/2) \Pr(N \in \exp(\lambda)S) + \frac{\delta}{2}.$$

(α, β)-Admissible noise distributions can be used to design (ϵ, δ)-differentially private mechanisms, as stated by the following theorem.

Theorem 8.18
Let N be an (α, β)-admissible noise distribution for (ϵ, δ)-differential privacy. Then the mechanism

$$\mathcal{A}(x) = f(x) + \frac{S_{f,\beta}(x)}{\alpha} N$$

gives (ϵ, δ)-differential privacy.

To come up with an effective mechanism for (ϵ, δ)-differential privacy we need an (α, β)-admissible noise distribution. Table 8.1 lists some noise distributions together with the levels of admissibility for (ϵ, δ)-differential privacy.

Table 8.1: Admissible distributions for (ϵ, δ)-differential privacy

Density function	(α, β)-admissibility for (ϵ, δ)
$\frac{1}{1+|z|^\gamma}$ for $\gamma > 1, z \in \mathbb{R}$	$(\frac{\epsilon}{4\gamma}, \frac{\epsilon}{\gamma})$
$\frac{1}{2}\exp(-|z|)$ for $z \in \mathbb{R}$	$(\frac{\epsilon}{2}, \frac{\epsilon}{2}\ln(\frac{1}{\delta}))$
$\frac{1}{2\pi}\exp(-\frac{z^2}{2})$ for $z \in \mathbb{R}$	$(\frac{\epsilon}{\sqrt{\ln(1/\delta)}}, \frac{\epsilon}{2}\ln(\frac{1}{\delta}))$

8.4   THE EXPONENTIAL MECHANISM

The mechanisms based on noise addition were designed for query functions f that take values in $\mathbb{R}^k$. When the outcome of the query is categorical rather than numerical these mechanisms may not be suitable. Ordinal categorical attributes can be seen as numerical attributes (for instance, by replacing each category by the corresponding rank) and, thus, the noise addition mechanisms remain useful. For other types of categorical attributes (e.g., nominal or hierarchical), where the relation between categories can be complex, trying to adapt previous mechanisms for numerical data is not an appropriate solution.

For a numerical query function it is implicit that the closer the value reported by the differentially private mechanism to the actual value the better. For categorical attributes, the effect on the utility of not getting the actual value must be clarified. This is done by introducing a scoring function that associates a score (utility) to each possible output given the actual data set.

Definition 8.19 Scoring function   Let $\mathcal{D}$ be the set of all possible data sets. Let $f : \mathcal{D} \to \mathcal{R}$ be a query function with values in a set $\mathcal{R}$. A scoring function u_f maps all pairs $(X, r) \in \mathcal{D} \times \mathcal{R}$ to a value in $\mathbb{R}$ showing how good r is as a replacement for $f(X)$. The greater $u_f(X, r)$ the better.

Having defined a scoring function that measures the relative utility of each possible response, we can design a differentially private mechanism that seeks to maximize the probability of the responses that give better utility [62].

Definition 8.20 The exponential mechanism   Given a scoring function $u_f : \mathcal{D} \times \mathcal{R} \to \mathbb{R}$, the exponential mechanism $\mathcal{E}^\epsilon_{u_f}$ evaluated at $X \in \mathcal{D}$ outputs a value in $r \in \mathcal{R}$ with probability proportional to $\exp(\frac{\epsilon}{2}u_f(X, r))$

$$\mathcal{E}^\epsilon_{u_f}(X) = \text{choose } r \text{ with probability proportional to } \exp(\tfrac{\epsilon}{2}u_f(X, r)).$$

It can be shown that the exponential mechanism gives $\epsilon \Delta u_f$-differential privacy, where Δu_f (the sensitivity of the scoring function) is the maximum change in the scoring function between neighbor data sets

$$\Delta u_f = \max_{\substack{d(X, X') = 1 \\ r \in \mathcal{R}}} |u_f(X, r) - u_f(X', r)|.$$

Theorem 8.21   The exponential mechanism $\mathcal{E}^{\epsilon}_{u_f}$ gives $\epsilon \Delta u_f$-differential privacy.

Although the exponential mechanism has been presented as a mechanism for categorical data, it is general enough to be applied for any kind of data. The scoring function models all the properties of the data that are of interest in trying to get the best response. For instance, the Laplace noise addition mechanism can be seen as an exponential mechanism with scoring function $u_f(X, r) = -|f(X) - r|$.

8.5   RELATION TO k-ANONYMITY-BASED MODELS

Syntactic privacy models are those models that require the protected data set to have a specific form that is known to offer protection against disclosure risk. In k-anonymity, we require the protected data set to be partitioned in equivalence classes with cardinality k or more. l-diversity and t-closeness add to the requirements of k-anonymity a minimum variability of the confidential attribute in each equivalence class. These privacy models are usually counterposed to differential privacy, which (instead of requiring the protected data set to have a specific form) limits the effect of any individual on a query response. However, [24, 91] show that t-closeness and differential privacy are more related than it may seem at first glance.

We show that, if t-closeness holds, then we have differential privacy on the projection over the confidential attributes. The quasi-identifier attributes are excluded from our discussion. The reason is that t-closeness offers no additional protection to the quasi-identifiers beyond what k-anonymity does. For example, we may learn that an individual is not in the data set if there is no equivalence class in the released t-close data whose quasi-identifier values are compatible with the individual's.

The main requirement for the implication between t-closeness and differential privacy relates to the satisfaction of the t-closeness requirements about the prior and posterior knowledge of an observer. t-closeness assumes that the distribution of the confidential data is public information (this is the prior view of observers about the confidential data) and limits the knowledge gain between the prior and posterior view (the distribution of the confidential data within the equivalence classes) by limiting the distance between both distributions.

Rather than using EMD as a distance for t-closeness, we consider the following multiplicative distance.

Definition 8.22   Given two random distributions D_1 and D_2, we define the distance between D_1 and D_2 as:

$$d(D_1, D_2) = \max\{\frac{\Pr_{D_1}(S)}{\Pr_{D_2}(S)}, \frac{\Pr_{D_2}(S)}{\Pr_{D_1}(S)}\}$$

where S is an arbitrary (measurable) set, and we take the quotients of probabilities to be zero, if both $\Pr_{D_1}(S)$ and $\Pr_{D_2}(S)$ are zero, and to be infinity if only one of them is zero.

If the distributions D_1 and D_2 are discrete (as is the case for the empirical distribution of a confidential attribute in a microdata set), computing the distance between them is simpler: taking the maximum over the possible individual values suffices.

Proposition 8.23 If distributions D_1 and D_2 take values in a discrete set $\{x_1, \ldots, x_n\}$, then the distance $d(D_1, D_2)$ can be computed as

$$d(D_1, D_2) = \max_{i=1,\ldots,n} \{\frac{\Pr_{D_1}(x_i)}{\Pr_{D_2}(x_i)}, \frac{\Pr_{D_2}(x_i)}{\Pr_{D_1}(x_i)}\}.$$

Suppose that t-closeness holds; that is, the protected data set Y consists of several equivalence classes selected in such a way that the multiplicative distance proposed in Definition 8.22 between the distribution of the confidential attribute over the whole data set and the distribution within each of the equivalence classes is less than t. We will show that, if the assumption on the prior and posterior views of the data made by t-closeness holds, then $\exp(\epsilon/2)$-closeness implies ϵ-differential privacy. A microdata release can be viewed as the collected answers to a set of queries, where each query requests the attribute values associated to a different individual. As the queries relate to different individuals, checking that differential privacy holds for each individual query suffices, by parallel composition, to check that it holds for the entire data set. Let I be a specific individual in the data set and let κ_I be the query that asks for I's confidential data. For differential privacy to hold, the response to κ_I should similar between data sets that differ in one record. Notice that, even if the response to query κ_I is associated with individual I, including I's data in the data set vs. not including them must modify the probability of the output by a factor not greater than $\exp(\epsilon)$. We have the following result.

Proposition 8.24 Let $\kappa_I(\cdot)$ be the function that, when evaluated on a data set, returns I's confidential data in the data set. If the assumptions of t-closeness hold, then $\exp(\epsilon/2)$-closeness implies ϵ-differential privacy of κ_I. In other words, if we restrict the domain of κ_I to $\exp(\epsilon/2)$-close data sets, then we have ϵ-differential privacy for κ_I.

Proof. Let Y_1 and Y_2 be data sets that differ in one record. We suppose that Y_1 and Y_2 satisfy $\exp(\epsilon/2)$-closeness. In other words, the distribution of the confidential data in each equivalence class of Y_i differs by a factor not greater than $\exp(\epsilon/2)$ from the prior knowledge, that is, the distribution of the confidential data in the overall Y_i, for $i = 1, 2$. We want to check that $\Pr(\kappa_I(Y_1) \in S) \le \exp(\epsilon) \Pr(\kappa_I(Y_2) \in S)$.

Let P_0 be the prior knowledge about the confidential data. The probabilities $\Pr(\kappa_I(Y_1) \in S)$ and $\Pr(\kappa_I(Y_2) \in S)$ are determined by the posterior view of I's confidential data given Y_1 and Y_2, respectively. We consider four different cases: (i) $I \notin Y_1$ and $I \notin Y_2$, (ii) $I \notin Y_1$ and $I \in Y_2$, (iii) $I \in Y_1$ and $I \notin Y_2$, and (iv) $I \in Y_1$ and $I \in Y_2$.

In case (i), the posterior view does not provide information about I beyond the one in the prior view: we have $\Pr(\kappa_I(Y_1) \in S) = P_0(S) = \Pr(\kappa_I(Y_2) \in S)$. Hence, the ϵ-differential privacy condition is satisfied.

Cases (ii) and (iii) are symmetric. We focus on case (ii). Because $I \notin Y_1$, the posterior view about I equals the prior view: $\Pr(\kappa_I(Y_1) \in S) = P_0(S)$. On the other hand, because $I \in Y_2$, the probability $\Pr(\kappa_I(Y_2) \in S)$ is determined by the distribution of the confidential data in the corresponding equivalence class (the posterior view). Because Y_2 satisfies $\exp(\epsilon/2)$-closeness the posterior view differs from the prior view by a factor of, at most, $\exp(\epsilon/2)$: $\Pr(\kappa_I(Y_2) \in S)/\Pr(\kappa_I(Y_1) \in S) \leq \exp(\epsilon/2)$. Hence, $\epsilon/2$-differential privacy condition is satisfied. In particular, ϵ-differential privacy condition is satisfied.

In case (iv), because $I \in Y_1$ and $I \in Y_2$, both probabilities $\Pr(\kappa_I(Y_1) \in S)$ and $\Pr(\kappa_I(Y_2) \in S)$ are determined by the corresponding posterior views. Because Y_1 and Y_2 satisfy $\exp(\epsilon/2)$-closeness, both posterior views differ from P_0 by a factor of not greater than $\exp(\epsilon/2)$. In particular, $\Pr(\kappa_I(Y_1) \in S)$ and $\Pr(\kappa_I(Y_2) \in S)$ differ at most by a factor of $\exp(\epsilon)$ and, hence, the ϵ-differential privacy condition is satisfied.   □

The previous proposition shows that, if the assumptions of t-closeness about the prior and posterior views of the intruder are satisfied, then the level of disclosure risk limitation provided by t-closeness is as good as the one of ϵ-differential privacy. Of course, differential privacy is independent of the prior knowledge, so the proposition does not apply in general. However, when it applies, it provides an effective way of generating an ϵ-differentially private data set, using the construction in [24].

8.6   DIFFERENTIALLY PRIVATE DATA PUBLISHING

In contrast to the general-purpose data publication offered by k-anonymity, which makes no assumptions on the uses of published data and does not limit the type and number of analyses that can be performed, *differential privacy severely limits data uses*. Indeed, in the interactive scenario, differential privacy allows only a limited number of queries to be answered (until the privacy budget is exhausted); in the extensions to the non-interactive scenario, any number of queries can be answered, but utility guarantees are only offered for a restricted class of queries.

The usual approach to releasing differentially private data sets is based on histogram queries [109, 110], that is, on approximating the data distribution by partitioning the data domain and counting the number of records in each partition set. To prevent the counts from leaking too much information, they are computed in a differentially private manner. Apart from the counts, partitioning can also reveal information. One way to prevent partitioning from leaking information consists in using a predefined partition that is independent of the actual data under consideration (e.g., by using a grid [54]).

The accuracy of the approximation obtained via histogram queries depends on the size of the histogram bins (the greater they are, the more imprecise is the attribute value) as well as on the number of records contained in them (the more records, the less relative error). For data sets with sparsely populated regions, using a predefined partition may be problematic. Several strategies have been proposed to improve the accuracy of differentially private count (histogram) queries, which we next review. In [42] consistency constraints between a set of queries are exploited to increase accuracy. In [108] a wavelet transform is performed on the data, and noise is added in the frequency domain. In [52, 110] the histogram bins are adjusted to the actual data. In [12], the authors consider differential privacy of attributes whose domain is ordered and has moderate to large cardinality (e.g., numerical attributes); the attribute domain is represented as a tree, which is decomposed in order to increase the accuracy of answers to count queries (multi-dimensional range queries). In [64], the authors generalize similar records by using coarser categories for the classification attributes; this results in higher counts of records in the histogram bins, which are much larger than the noise that needs to be added to reach differential privacy. For data sets with a significant number of attributes, attaining differential privacy while at the same time preserving the accuracy of the attribute values (by keeping the histogram bins small enough) becomes a complex task. Observe that, given a number of bins per attribute, the total number of bins grows exponentially with the number of attributes. Thus, in order to avoid obtaining too many sparsely populated bins, the number of bins per attribute must be significantly reduced (with the subsequent accuracy loss).

An interesting approach to deal with multidimensional data is proposed in [63, 111]. The goal of these papers is to compute differentially private histograms independently for each attribute (or jointly for a small number of attributes) and then try to generate a joint histogram for all attributes from the partial histograms. This was done for a data set of commuting patterns in [63] and for an arbitrary data set in [111]. In particular, [111] first tried to build a dependency hierarchy between attributes. Intuitively, when two attributes are independent, their joint histogram can be reconstructed from the histograms of each of the attributes; thus, the dependency hierarchy helps determine which marginal or low-dimension histograms are more interesting to approximate the joint histogram.

An alternative to the generation of differentially private synthetic data sets via histogram approximation is to apply a masking procedure to the records in the original data set. We can see the process of generation of the differentially private data set as the process of giving differentially private answers to the queries that ask for the contents of each record. Of course, since the purpose of differential privacy is to make the answer to a query similar independently of the presence or absence of any individual, if the generation of the differentially private data set is done naively a large information loss can be expected. Two approaches based on microaggregation have been proposed to reduce the sensitivity of the queries. In [96, 97] a multivariate microaggregation is run on the original data and the differentially private data set is generated from the centroids of microaggregation clusters. Since the centroid is the average of all records in the cluster, it is less sensitive than a single record. The multivariate microaggregation approach is presented in

Chapter 9.3. In [85, 86] a univariate microaggregation is performed on each attribute in order to offer better utility preservation.

8.7 SUMMARY

This chapter has introduced the (ϵ, δ)-differential privacy model, as well as its better-known particular case ϵ-differential privacy. Unlike k-anonymity, l-diversity, and t-closeness, that were aimed at microdata releases, differential privacy seeks to guarantee that the response to a query is not disclosive (by guaranteeing that the presence or absence of any individual does not substantially modify the query response). Three types of mechanisms to attain differential privacy have been presented: data-independent noise addition (which adds an amount of noise that is independent of the actual data set), data-dependent noise addition (which adds an amount of noise that depends on the actual data set), and the exponential mechanism (which is based on a scoring function that rates the utility of each possible result). We have also shown that, if the assumptions of t-closeness are satisfied, the level of protection provided by t-closeness is comparable to the level of protection offered by ϵ-differential privacy. Although not initially intended for microdata releases, differentially private data sets may be generated. We have introduced two approaches to this task: i) via histogram queries, that is, via a differentially private approximation of the original data, and ii) via perturbative masking yielding differentially private responses to the queries that ask for the contents of each record. In the next two chapters, we describe in detail two microaggregation-based mechanisms aimed at reducing the noise that needs to be added to obtain differentially private data sets.

CHAPTER 9

Differential Privacy by Multivariate Microaggregation

Although differential privacy was designed as a privacy model for queryable databases, as introduced in Section 8.6, several methods to generate differentially private data sets have been proposed. This chapter reviews perturbative masking approaches to generate a differentially private data set aimed at being as general as k-anonymity [96, 97].

9.1 REDUCING SENSITIVITY VIA PRIOR MULTIVARIATE MICROAGGREGATION

Differential privacy and microaggregation offer quite different disclosure limitation guarantees. Differential privacy is introduced in a query-response environment and offers probabilistic guarantees that the contribution of any single individual to the query response is limited, while microaggregation is used to protect microdata releases and works by clustering groups of individuals and replacing them by the group centroid. When applied to the quasi-identifier attributes, microaggregation achieves k-anonymity. In spite of those differences, we can leverage the masking introduced by microaggregation to decrease the amount of random noise required to attain differential privacy.

Let X be a data set with attributes $X^1, \ldots, X^m$ and $\bar{X}$ be a microaggregated X with minimal cluster size k. Let M be a microaggregation function that takes as input a data set, and outputs a microaggregated version of it: $M(X) = \bar{X}$. Let f be an arbitrary query function for which an ϵ-differentially private response is requested. A typical differentially private mechanism takes these steps: capture the query f, compute the real response $f(X)$, and output a masked value $f(X) + N$, where N is a random noise whose magnitude is adjusted to the sensitivity of f.

To improve the utility of an ϵ-differentially private response to f, we seek to minimize the distortion introduced by the random noise N. Two main approaches are used for this purpose. In the first one, a random noise is used that allows for a finer calibration to the query f under consideration. For instance, if the variability of the query f is highly dependent on the actual data set X, using a data-dependent noise (like in Section 8.3) would probably reduce the magnitude of the noise. In the second approach, the query function f is modified so that the new query function is less sensitive to modifications of a record in the data set.

The use of microaggregation proposed in this chapter falls into the second approach: we replace the original query function f by $f \circ M$, that is, we run the query f over the microaggregated data set $\bar{X}$. For our proposal to be meaningful, the function $f \circ M$ must be a good approximation of f. Our assumption is that the microaggregated data set $\bar{X}$ preserves the statistical information contained in the original data set X; therefore, any query that is only concerned with the statistical properties of the data in X can be run over the microaggregated data set $\bar{X}$ without much deviation. The function $f \circ M$ will certainly not be a good approximation of f when the output of f depends on the properties of specific individuals; however, this is not our case, as we are only interested in the extraction of statistical information.

Since the k-anonymous data set $\bar{X}$ is formed by the centroids of the clusters (i.e., the average records), for the sensitivity of the queries $f \circ M$ to be effectively reduced the centroid must be stable against modifications of one record in the original data set X. This means that modification of one record in the original data set X should only slightly affect the centroids in the microaggregated data set. Although this will hold for most of the clusters yielded by any microaggregation algorithm, we need it to hold for all clusters in order to effectively reduce the sensitivity.

Not all microaggregation algorithms satisfy the above requirement; for instance, if the microaggregation algorithm could generate a completely unrelated set of clusters after modification of a single record in X, the effect on the centroids could be large. As we are modifying one record in X, the best we can expect is a set of clusters that differ in one record from the original set of clusters. Microaggregation algorithms with this property lead to the greatest reduction in the query sensitivity; we refer to them as insensitive microaggregation algorithms.

Definition 9.1 (Insensitive microaggregation). Let X be a data set, M a microaggregation algorithm, and let $\{C_1, \ldots, C_n\}$ be the set of clusters that result from running M on X. Let X' be a data set that differs from X in a single record, and $\{C'_1, \ldots, C'_n\}$ be the clusters produced by running M on X'. We say that M is insensitive to the input data if, for every pair of data sets X and X' differing in a single record, there is a bijection between the set of clusters $\{C_1, \ldots, C_n\}$ and the set of clusters $\{C'_1, \ldots, C'_n\}$ such that each pair of corresponding clusters differs at most in a single record.

Since for an insensitive microaggregation algorithm corresponding clusters differ at most in one record, bounding the variability of the centroid is simple. For instance, for numerical data, when computing the centroid as the mean, the maximum change for each attribute equals the size of the range of the attribute divided by k. If the microaggregation was not insensitive, a single modification in X might lead to completely different clusters, and hence to large variability in the centroids.

The output of microaggregation algorithms is usually highly dependent on the input data. On the positive side, this leads to greater within-cluster homogeneity and hence less information loss. On the negative side, modifying a single record in the input data may lead to completely different clusters; in other words, such algorithms are not insensitive to the input data as per Definition 9.1. We illustrate this fact for MDAV. Figure 9.1 shows the clusters generated by MDAV for a toy data set X consisting of 15 records with two attributes, before and after modifying a single record. In MDAV, we use the Euclidean distance and $k = 5$. Two of the clusters in the original data set differ by more than one record from the respective most similar clusters in the modified data set. Therefore, no mapping between clusters of both data sets exists that satisfies the requirements of Definition 9.1. The centroids of the clusters are represented by a cross. A large change in the centroids between the original and the modified data sets can be observed.

We want to turn MDAV into an insensitive microaggregation algorithm, so that it can be used as the microaggregation algorithm to generate $\bar{X}$. MDAV depends on two parameters: the minimal cluster size k, and the distance function d used to measure the distance between records. Modifying k does not help making MDAV insensitive: similar examples to the ones in Figure 9.1 can easily be proposed for any $k > 1$; on the other hand, setting $k = 1$ does make MDAV insensitive, but it is equivalent to not performing any microaggregation at all. Next, we see that MDAV is insensitive if the distance function d is consistent with a total order relation.

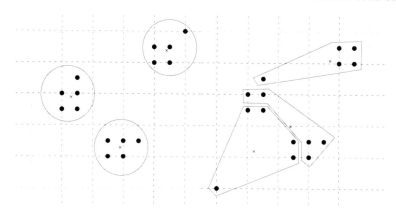

Figure 9.1: MDAV clusters and centroids with $k = 5$. Left, original data set X; right, data set after modifying one record in X.

Definition 9.2   A distance function $d : X \times X \rightarrow \mathbb{R}$ is said to be consistent with an order relation $\leq_X$ if $d(x, y) \leq d(x, z)$ whenever $x \leq_X y \leq_X z$.

Proposition 9.3   Let X be a data set equipped with a total order relation $\leq_X$. Let $d : X \times X \rightarrow \mathbb{R}$ be a distance function consistent with $\leq_X$. MDAV with distance d satisfies the insensitivity condition (Definition 9.1).

Proof. When the distance d is consistent with a total order, MDAV with cluster size k reduces to iteratively taking sets with cardinality k from the extremes, until less than k records are left;

the remaining records form the last cluster. Let $x_1, \ldots, x_n$ be the elements of X sorted according to $\leq_X$. MDAV generates a set of clusters of the form:

$$\{x_1, \ldots, x_k\}, \ldots, \{x_{n-k+1}, \ldots, x_n\}.$$

We want to check that modifying a single record of X leads to a set of clusters that differ in at most one element. Suppose that we modify record x by setting it to x', and let X' be the modified data set. Without loss of generality, we assume that $x \leq_X x'$; the proof is similar for the case $x' \leq_X x$.

Let C be the cluster of X that contains x, and C' the cluster of X' that contains x'. Let m be the minimum of the elements in C, and let M be the maximum of the elements in C'. As MDAV takes groups of k records from the extremes, the clusters of X whose elements are all inferior to m, or all superior to M remain unmodified in X'. Therefore, we can assume that x belongs to the leftmost cluster of X, and x' belongs to the rightmost cluster in X'.

Let $C_1, \ldots, C_m$ and $C'_1, \ldots, C'_m$ be, respectively, the clusters of X and X', ordered according to $\leq_X$. Let x^i_1 and $x^i_{j_i}$ be the minimum and the maximum of the elements of C_i: $C_i = \{z \in X \mid x^i_1 \leq_X z \leq_X x^i_{j_i}\}$. Cluster C'_1 contains the same elements as C_1 except for x that has been removed from C'_1 and for x^2_1 that has been added to C'_1, $C'_1 = (C_1 \cup \{x^2_1\}) \setminus \{x\}$. Clusters $C'_2, \ldots, C'_{m-1}$ contain the same elements as the respective cluster $C_2, \ldots, C_{m-1}$, except for x^i_1 that has been removed from C'_i and x^{i+1}_1 that has been added to C'_i. Cluster C'_m contains the same elements as C_m except for x^m_1 that has been removed from C'_m and x' that has been added to C'_m. Therefore, clusters C_i and C'_i differ in a single record for all i, which completes the proof. $\square$

We have seen that, when the distance function is consistent with a total order relation, MDAV is insensitive. Now, we want to determine the necessary conditions for an arbitrary microaggregation algorithm to be insensitive. Algorithm 7 describes the general form of a microaggregation algorithm with fixed cluster size k. Essentially it keeps selecting groups of k records, until fewer than $2k$ records are left; the remaining records form the last cluster, whose size is between k and $2k - 1$. Generating each cluster requires a selection criterion to prioritize some elements over the others. We can think of this prioritization as an order relation $\leq_i$, and the selection criterion for constructing the cluster C_i to be "select the k smallest records according to $\leq_i$." Note that the prioritization used to generate different clusters need not be the same; for instance, MDAV selects the remaining element that is farthest from the average of remaining points, and prioritizes based on the distance to it.

Let X and X' be a pair of data sets that differ in one record. For Algorithm 7 to be insensitive, the sequence of orders $\leq_i$ must be constant across executions of the algorithm; to see this, note that if one of the orders $\leq_i$ changed, we could easily construct data sets X and X' such that cluster C_i in X would differ by more than one record from its corresponding cluster in X', and hence the algorithm would not be insensitive.

Algorithm 7 General form of a microaggregation algorithm with fixed cluster size

---

let X be the original data set
let k be the minimal cluster size

set $i := 0$
while $|X| \geq 2k$ **do**
    $C_i \leftarrow k$ smallest elements from X according to $\leq_i$
    $X := X \setminus C_i$
    $i := i + 1$
end while
$\overline{X} \leftarrow$ Replace each record $r \in X$ by the centroid of its cluster

return $\overline{X}$

Another requirement for Algorithm 7 to be insensitive is that the priority assigned by $\leq_i$ to any two different elements must be different. If there were different elements sharing the same priority, we could end up with clusters that differ by more than one record. For instance, assume that the sets X and X' are such that $X' = (X \cup \{x\}) \setminus \{x'\}$, and assume that x belongs to cluster C_i and x' belongs to cluster C_i'. Clusters C_i and C_i' already differ in one element, so for the clustering to be insensitive all the other records in these clusters must be equal. If there was a pair of elements, $y \neq y'$, with the same priority, and if only one of them was included in each of the clusters C_i and C_i', then, as there is no way to discriminate between y and y', we could, for instance, include y in C_i, and y' in C_i'. In that case the clusters C_i and C_i' would differ by more than one record. Therefore, for the microaggregation to be insensitive $\leq_i$ must assign a different priority to each element; in other words, $\leq_i$ must be a total order.

A similar argument to the one used in Proposition 9.3 can be used to show that when the total order relation is the same for all the clusters—in other words, when $\leq_i$ and $\leq_j$ are equal for any i and j—then Algorithm 7 is insensitive to the input data. However, we want to show that even when the total orders $\leq_i$ are different, insensitivity still holds. In fact, Proposition 9.4 provides a complete characterization of insensitive microaggregation algorithms of the form of Algorithm 7.

Proposition 9.4   Algorithm 7 is insensitive to input data if and only if $\{\leq_i\}_{i \in \mathbb{N}}$ is a fixed sequence of total order relations defined over the domain of X.

Proof. In the discussion previous to Proposition 9.3 we have already shown that if Algorithm 7 is insensitive, then $\{\leq_i\}_{i \in \mathbb{N}}$ must be a fixed sequence of total order relations. We show now that the reverse implication also holds: if $\{\leq_i\}_{i \in \mathbb{N}}$ is a fixed sequence of total order relations, then Algorithm 7 is insensitive to input data.

Let X and X' be, respectively, the original data set and a data set that differs from X in one record. Let C_i and C_i' be, respectively, the clusters generated at step i for the data sets X and X'. We want to show, for any i, that C_i and C_i' differ in at most one record.

An argument similar to the one in Proposition 9.3 shows that the clusters C_0 and C_0' that result from the first iteration of the algorithm differ in at most one record. To see that Algorithm 7 is insensitive, it is enough to check that the sets $X \setminus C_0$ and $X' \setminus C_0'$ differ in at most one record; then, we could apply the previous argument to $X \setminus C_0$ and $X' \setminus C_0'$ to see that C_1 and C_1' differ in one record, and so on.

Let $x_1, \ldots, x_n$ be the elements of X ordered according to $\leq_0$, so that $C_0 = \{x_1, \ldots, x_k\}$. Assume that X' has had element x replaced by x': $X' = \{x_1, \ldots, x_n, x'\} \setminus \{x\}$. We have the following four possibilities. (i) If neither x belongs to C_0 nor x' belongs to C_0', then C_0 and C_0' must be equal; therefore, $X \setminus C_0$ and $X' \setminus C_0'$ differ, at most, in one record. (ii) If both x belongs to C_0 and x' belongs to C_0', then $X \setminus C_0$ and $X' \setminus C_0'$ are equal. (iii) If x belongs to C_0 but x' does not belong to C_0', we can write C_0' as $\{x_1, \ldots, x_{k+1}\} \setminus \{x\}$; the set $X' \setminus C_0'$ is $\{x_{k+2}, \ldots, x_n, x'\}$, which differs in one record from $X \setminus C_0 = \{x_{k+1}, \ldots, x_n\}$; and (iv) If x is not in C_0 but x' is in C_0', we can write C_0' as $\{x_1, \ldots, x_{k-1}, x'\}$; the set $X' \setminus C_0'$ is $\{x_k, \ldots, x_n\} \setminus \{x\}$, which differs in one record from $X \setminus C_0 = \{x_{k+1}, \ldots, x_n\}$. Therefore, we have seen that $X \setminus C_0$ and $X' \setminus C_0'$ differ in at most one record, which completes the proof.   □

Using multiple order relations in Algorithm 7, as allowed by Proposition 9.4, in contrast with the single order relation used to turn MDAV insensitive in Proposition 9.3, allows us to increase the within-cluster homogeneity achieved in the microaggregation.

The modification of the query function f to $f \circ M$ by introducing a prior microaggregation step is intended to reduce the sensitivity of the query function. Assume that the microaggregation function f computes the centroid of each cluster as the mean of its components. We analyze next how microaggregation affects the L_1-sensitivity of the query function f.

The L_1-sensitivity of f, $\Delta(f)$, measures the maximum change in f that results from a modification of a single record in X. Essentially, the microaggregation step M in $f \circ M$ distributes the modification suffered by a single record in X among multiple records in $M(X)$. Consider, for instance, the data sets X and X' depicted in Figure 9.2. The record at the top right corner in X has been moved to the bottom left corner in X'; all the other records remain unmodified. In the microaggregated data sets $M(X)$ and $M(X')$—the crosses represent the centroids—we observe that all the centroids have been modified but the magnitude of the modifications is smaller: the modification suffered by the record at the top right corner of X has been distributed among all the records in $M(X)$.

When computing the centroid as the mean, we can guarantee that the maximum variation in any centroid is at most $1/k$ of the variation of the record in X. Therefore, we can think of the L_1-sensitivity of $f \circ M$ as the maximum change in f if we allow a variation in each record that is less than $1/k$ times the maximal variation. In fact, this is a very rough estimate, as only a few centroids can have a variation equaling $1/k$ of the maximal variation in X, but it is useful to analyze some simple functions such as the identity. The identity function returns the exact contents of a specific record, and is used extensively in later sections to construct ϵ-differentially private data sets. The sensitivity of the identity functions depends only on the maximum variation that the selected record may suffer; therefore, it is clear that distributing the variation among several records decreases sensitivity. This is formalized in the following proposition.

Proposition 9.5 Let $X \in D^n$ be a data set with numerical attributes only. Let M be a microaggregation function with minimal cluster size k that computes the centroid by taking the mean of the elements of each cluster. Given a record $r \in X$, let $I_r()$ be the function that returns the attribute values contained in record r of X. Then $\Delta(I_r \circ M) \leq \Delta(I_r)/k$.

Proof. The function $I_r \circ M$ returns the centroid of $M(X)$ that corresponds to the record r in X. It was shown in the discussion that precedes the proposition that, for a data set that contains only numerical attributes, if the centroid is computed as the mean of the records in the cluster, then the maximum change in any centroid is, at most, $\Delta(I_r)/k$; that is, $\Delta(I_r \circ M) \leq \Delta(I_r)/k$.   □

9.2   DIFFERENTIALLY PRIVATE DATA SETS BY INSENSITIVE MICROAGGREGATION

Assume that we have an original data set X and that we want to generate a data set X_ϵ—an anonymized version of X—that satisfies ϵ-differential privacy. Even if differential privacy was not introduced with the aim of generating anonymized data sets, we can think of a data release as the collected answers to successive queries for each record in the data set. Let $I_r()$ be as defined in Proposition 9.5. We generate X_ϵ, by querying X with $I_r(X)$, for all $r \in X$. If the responses to the queries $I_r()$ satisfy ϵ-differential privacy, then, as each query refers to a different record, by the parallel composition property X_ϵ also satisfies ϵ-differential privacy.

The proposed approach for generating X_ϵ is general but naive. As each query $I_r()$ refers to a single individual, its sensitivity is large; therefore, the masking required to attain ϵ-differential privacy is quite significant, and thus the utility of such an X_ϵ very limited.

To improve the utility of X_ϵ, we introduce a microaggregation step as discussed in Section 9.1: (i) from the original data set X, we generate a k-anonymous data set $\overline{X}$—by using a microaggregation algorithm with minimum cluster size k, like MDAV, and assuming that all attributes are quasi-identifiers—and (ii) the ϵ-differentially private data set X_ϵ is generated from the k-anonymous data set $\overline{X}$ by taking an ϵ-differentially private response to the queries $I_r(\overline{X})$, for all $r \in \overline{X}$.

By constructing the k-anonymous data set $\overline{X}$, we stop thinking in terms of individuals, to start thinking in terms of groups of k individuals. Now, the sensitivity of the queries $I_r(\overline{X})$ used to construct X_ϵ reflects the effect that modifying a single record in X has on the groups of k records in $\overline{X}$. The fact that each record in $\overline{X}$ depends on k (or more) records in X is what allows the sensivity to be effectively reduced. See Proposition 9.5 above.

Algorithm 8 details the procedure for generating the differentially private data set X_ϵ.

Algorithm 8 Generation of an ϵ-differentially private data set X_ϵ from X via microaggregation

---

let X be the original data set
let M be an insensitive microaggregation algorithm with minimal cluster size k
let $S_\epsilon()$ be an ϵ-differentially private sanitizer
let $I_r()$ be the query for the attributes of record r

$\overline{X} \leftarrow$ microaggregated data set $M(X)$
for each $r \in \overline{X}$ **do**
　　$r_\epsilon \leftarrow S_\epsilon(I_r(\overline{X}))$
　　insert r_ϵ into X_ϵ
end for

return X_ϵ

Achieving differential privacy with numerical attributes

For a data set consisting of numerical attributes only, generating the ϵ-differentially private data set X_ϵ as previously described is quite straightforward.

Let X be a data set with m numerical attributes: $X^1, \ldots, X^m$. The first step to construct X_ϵ is to generate the k-anonymous data set $\overline{X}$ via an insensitive microaggregation algorithm. As we have seen in Section 9.1, the key point of insensitive microaggregation algorithms is to define a total order relation over $Dom(X)$, the domain of the records of the data set X. The domain of X contains all the possible values that make sense, given the semantics of the attributes. In other words, the domain is not defined by the actual records in X but by the set of values that make sense for each attribute and by the relation between attributes.

Microaggregation algorithms use a distance function, $d : Dom(X) \times Dom(X) \rightarrow \mathbb{R}$, to measure the distances between records and generate the clusters. We assume that such a distance function is already available and we define a total order with which the distance is consistent. To construct a total order, we take a reference point R, and define the order according to the distance to R. Given a pair of elements $x, y \in Dom(X)$, we say that $x \leq y$ if $d(R, x) \leq d(R, y)$. On the other hand, we still need to define the relation between elements that are equally distant from R. As we assume that the data set X consists of numerical attributes only, we can take advantage of the fact that individual attributes are equipped with a total order—the usual numerical order—and sort the records that are equally distant from R by means of the alphabetical order: given $x = (x_1, \ldots, x_m)$ and $y = (y_1, \ldots, y_m)$, with $d(x, R) = d(y, R)$, we say that $x \leq y$ if $(x_1, \ldots, x_m) \leq (y_1, \ldots, y_m)$ according to the alphabetical order.

Proposition 9.5 shows that, as a result of the insensitive microaggregation, one has $\Delta(I_r \circ M) = \Delta(I_r)/k$; therefore, ϵ-differential privacy can be achieved by adding to $\overline{X}$ an amount of Laplace noise that would only achieve $k\epsilon$-differential privacy if directly added to X.

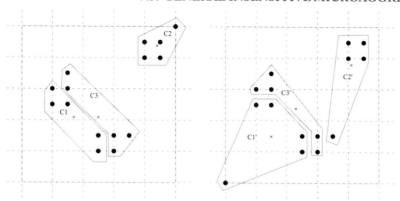

Figure 9.2: Insensitive MDAV microaggregation with $k = 5$. Left, original data set X; right, data set after modifying one record in X.

Insensitive MDAV

According to Proposition 9.3, to make MDAV insensitive we must define a total order among the elements in $Dom(X)$. According to the previous discussion, this total order is constructed by selecting a reference point. To increase within-cluster homogeneity, MDAV starts by clustering the elements at the boundaries. For our total order to follow this guideline, the reference point R must be selected among the elements of the boundary of $Dom(X)$. For instance, if the domain of X^i is $[a_b^i, a_t^i]$, we can set R to be the point $(a_b^1, \dots, a_b^m)$.

Figure 9.2 illustrates the insensitive microaggregation obtained by using MDAV with the total order defined above. The original data set X and the modified data set X' are the same of Figure 9.1. We also use $k = 5$ and the Euclidean distance for insensitive MDAV. Let us take as the reference point for the above defined total order the point R at the lower left corner of the grids. Note that now clusters C_1, C_2, and C_3 in X differ in a single record from C_1', C_2', and C_3' in X', respectively. By comparing Figures 9.1 and 9.2, we observe that the standard (non-insensitive) MDAV results in a set of clusters with greater within-cluster homogeneity; however, in exchange for the lost homogeneity, insensitive MDAV generates sets of clusters that are more stable when one record of the data set changes.

9.3   GENERAL INSENSITIVE MICROAGGREGATION

It was seen in Section 9.1 that each clustering step within microaggregation can use a different total order relation, as long as the sequence of order relations is kept constant. The advantage of using multiple total order relations is that it allows the insensitive microaggregation algorithm to better mimic a standard non-insensitive microaggregation algorithm, and thus increase the within-cluster homogeneity.

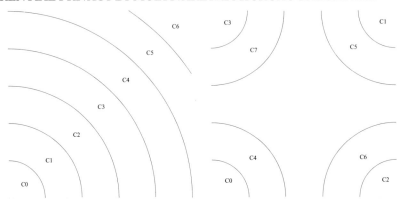

Figure 9.3: Cluster formation. Left, using a single reference point; right, taking each corner of the domain as a reference point.

The sequence of total orders is determined by a sequence of reference points R_i. In the selection of R_i we try to match the criteria used by non-insensitive microaggregation algorithms to increase within-cluster homogeneity: start clustering at the boundaries, and generate a cluster that is far apart from the previously generated cluster.

Let the domain of X^i be $[a_b^i, a_t^i]$. Define the set $\mathcal{R}$ of candidate reference points at those points in the boundaries of $Dom(X)$, that is:

$$\mathcal{R} = \{(a_{v_1}^1, \ldots, a_{v_m}^m)|v_i \in \{b, t\} \text{ for } 1 \leq i \leq m\}.$$

The first reference point R_1 is arbitrarily selected from $\mathcal{R}$; for instance, $R_1 = (a_b^1, \ldots, a_b^m)$. Once a point R_i has been selected, R_{i+1} is selected among the still unselected points in $\mathcal{R}$ so that it maximizes the Hamming distance to R_i—if $R_1 = (a_b^1, \ldots, a_b^m)$, then $R_2 = (a_t^1, \ldots, a_t^m)$. If several unselected points in $\mathcal{R}$ maximize the Hamming distance to R_i, we select the one among them with greatest distance to R_{i-1}, and so on.

Figure 9.3 shows the form of the clusters for a data set containing two numerical attributes. The graphic on the left is for a single reference point—this is also the form of the clusters obtained by insensitive MDAV, which uses a single total order relation. The graphic on the right uses four reference points, one for each edge of the domain, which are selected in turns as described above.

9.4   DIFFERENTIAL PRIVACY WITH CATEGORICAL ATTRIBUTES

Many data sets contain attributes with categorical values, such as Race, Country of birth, or Job [67]. Unlike continuous-scale numerical attributes, categorical attributes take values from a finite set of categories for which the arithmetical operations needed to microaggregate and add noise to the outputs do not make sense. In the sequel, we detail alternative mechanisms that are suitable for categorical attributes in order to achieve differential privacy as detailed above.

Let X be a data set with m categorical attributes: $X^1, \ldots, X^m$. The first challenge regards the definition of $Dom(X)$. Unlike for numerical attributes, the universe of each categorical attribute can only be defined by extension, listing all the possible values. This universe can be expressed either as a flat list or it can be structured in a hierarchic/taxonomic way. The latter scenario is more desirable, since the taxonomy implicitly captures the semantics inherent to conceptualizations of categorical values (e.g., disease categories, job categories, sports categories, etc.). In this manner, further operations can exploit this taxonomic knowledge to provide a semantically coherent management of attribute values [57].

Formally, a taxonomy τ can be defined as an upper semilattice $\leq_\varsigma$ on a set of concepts ς with a top element $root_\varsigma$. We define the taxonomy $\tau(X^i)$ associated to an attribute X^i as the lattice on the minimum set of concepts that covers all values in $Dom(X^i)$. Notice that $\tau(X^i)$ will include all values in $Dom(X^i)$ (e.g., "skiing," "sailing," "swimming," "soccer," etc., if the attribute refers to sport names) and, usually, some additional generalizations that are necessary to define the taxonomic structure (e.g.,"winter sports," "water sports," "field sports," and "sport" as the *root* of the taxonomy).

If $X^1, \ldots, X^m$ are independent attributes, $Dom(X)$ can be defined as the ordered combination of values of each $Dom(X^i)$, as modeled in their corresponding taxonomies $\tau(X^i), \ldots, \tau(X^m)$. If $X^1, \ldots, X^m$ are not independent, value tuples in $Dom(X)$ may be restricted to a subset of valid combinations.

Next, a suitable distance function $d : Dom(X) \times Dom(X) \to \mathbb{R}$ to compare records should be defined. To tackle this problem, we can exploit the taxonomy $\tau(X^i)$ associated with each X^i in X and the notion of *semantic distance* [84]. A semantic distance δ quantifies the amount of semantic differences observed between two terms (i.e., categorical values) according to the knowledge modeled in a taxonomy. Section 9.5 discusses the adequacy of several semantic measures in the context of differential privacy. By composing semantic distances δ for individual attributes X^i, each one computed from the corresponding taxonomy $\tau(X^i)$, we can define the required distance $d : Dom(X) \times Dom(X) \to \mathbb{R}$.

To construct a total order that yields insensitive and within-cluster homogeneous microaggregation as detailed in Section 9.3, we need to define the boundaries of $Dom(X)$, from which records will be clustered. Unlike in the numerical case, this is not straightforward since most categorical attributes are not ordinal and, hence, a total order cannot be trivially defined even for individual attributes. However, since the taxonomy $\tau(X^i)$ models the domain of X^i, boundaries of $Dom(X^i)$, that is, $[a_b^i, a_t^i]$, can be defined as the most distant and opposite values from the "middle" of $\tau(X^i)$. From a semantic perspective, this notion of centrality in a taxonomy can be measured by the *marginality model* [23]. This model determines the central point of the taxonomy and how far each value is from that center, according to the semantic distance between value pairs.

The *marginality* $m(\cdot,\cdot)$ of each value a_j^i in X^i with respect to its domain of values $Dom(X^i)$ is computed as

$$m(Dom(X^i),a_j^i) = \sum_{a_l^i \in Dom(X^i)-\{a_j^i\}} \delta(a_l^i,a_j^i) \tag{9.1}$$

where $\delta(\cdot,\cdot)$ is the semantic distance between two values. The greater $m(Dom(X^i),a_j^i)$, the more marginal (i.e., the less central) is a_j^i with regard to $Dom(X^i)$.

Hence, for each X^i, one boundary a_b^i of $Dom(X^i)$ can be defined as the most marginal value of $Dom(X^i)$:

$$a_b^i = \arg\max_{a_j^i \in Dom(A_i)} m(Dom(X^i),a_j^i). \tag{9.2}$$

The other boundary a_t^i can be defined as the most distant value from a_b^i in $Dom(X^i)$:

$$a_t^i = \arg\max_{a_j^i \in Dom(A_i)} \delta(a_j^i,a_b^i). \tag{9.3}$$

By applying the above expressions to the set of attributes $X^1,\ldots,X^m$ in X, the set $\mathcal{R}$ of candidate reference points needed to define a total order according to the semantic distance can be constructed as described in Section 9.3.

If no taxonomic structure is available, other centrality measures based on data distribution can be used (e.g., by selecting the modal value as the most central value [26]). However, such measures omit data semantics and result in significantly less useful anonymized results [57].

Similarly to the numerical case, if several records are equally distant from the reference points, the alphabetical criterion can be used to induce an order within those equidistant records.

At this point, records in X can be grouped using the insensitive microaggregation algorithm, thereby yielding a set of clusters with a sensitivity of only one record per cluster. The elements in each cluster must be replaced by the cluster centroid (i.e., the arithmetical mean in the numerical case) in order to obtain a k-anonymous data set. Since the mean of a sample of categorical values cannot be computed in the standard arithmetical sense, we rely again on the notion of marginality [23]: the mean of a sample of categorical values can be approximated by the least marginal value in the taxonomy, which is taken as the *centroid* of the set.

Formally, given a sample $S(X^i)$ of a nominal attribute X^i in a certain cluster, the marginality-based centroid for that cluster is defined in [23] as:

$$Centroid(S(X^i)) = \arg\min_{a_j^i \in \tau(S(A_i))} m(S(X^i),a_j^i) \tag{9.4}$$

where $\tau(S(X^i))$ is the minimum taxonomy extracted from $\tau(X^i)$ that includes all values in $S(X^i)$. Notice that by considering as centroid candidates all concepts in $\tau(S(X^i))$, which include all values in $S(X^i)$ and also their taxonomic generalizations, we improve the numerical accuracy of the centroid discretization inherent to categorical attributes [57].

The numerical value associated with each centroid candidate a_j^i corresponds to its marginality value $m(S(X^i), a_j^i)$, which depends on the sample of values in the cluster. Given a cluster of records with a set of independent attributes $X^1, \ldots, X^m$, the cluster centroid can be obtained by composing the individual centroids of each attribute.

As in the numerical case, cluster centroids depend on input data. To fulfill differential privacy for categorical attributes, two aspects must be considered. On the one hand, the centroid computation should evaluate as centroid candidates all the values in the taxonomy associated to the *domain* of each attribute ($\tau(X^i)$), and not only the sample of values to be aggregated ($\tau(S(X^i))$), since the centroid should be insensitive to any value change of input data within the attribute's domain. On the other hand, to achieve insensitivity, uncertainty must be added to the centroid computation. Since adding Laplacian noise to centroids makes no sense for categorical values, an alternative way to obtain differentially private outputs consists in selecting centroids in a probabilistic manner. The general idea is to select centroids with a degree of uncertainty that is proportional to the suitability of each centroid and the desired degree of ϵ-differential privacy. To do so, the Exponential Mechanism [62] can be applied. As introduced in Section 8.4, given a function with discrete outputs t, the mechanism chooses the output that is close to the optimum according to the input data D and quality criterion $q(D, t)$, while preserving ϵ-differential privacy.

Based on the above arguments, ϵ-differentially private centroids can be selected as indicated in Algorithm 9.

Algorithm 9 Computation of ϵ-differentially private centroids for clusters with categorical attributes

---

let C be a cluster with at least k records

for each categorical attribute X^i **do**
    Take as quality criterion $q(\cdot, \cdot)$ for each centroid candidate a_j^i in $\tau(X^i)$ the additive inverse of its marginality toward the attribute values $S(X^i)$ contained in C, that is, $-m(S(X^i), a_j^i)$;
    Sample the centroid from a distribution that assigns

$$\Pr(a_j^i) \propto \exp(\frac{\epsilon \times (-m(S(X^i), a_j^i))}{2\Delta(m(X^i))}) \tag{9.5}$$

end for

Notice that the inversion of the marginality function has no influence on the relative probabilities of centroid candidates, since it is achieved through a *bijective linear transformation*.

With the algorithm we have the following result, which is parallel to what we saw in the numerical case: if the input data are k-anonymous, the higher k, the less the uncertainty that needs to be added to reach ϵ-differential privacy.

Proposition 9.6   Let X be a data set with categorical attributes. Let $\overline{X}$ be a k-anonymous version of X generated using an insensitive microaggregation algorithm M with minimum cluster size k. ϵ-differential privacy can be achieved by using Algorithm 9 to obtain cluster centroids in $\overline{X}$ with an amount of uncertainty that decreases as k grows.

Proof. Without loss of generality, we can write the proof for a single attribute X^i. The argument can be composed for multi-attribute data sets.

Let $\Delta(m(X^i))$ be the sensitivity of the marginality function for attribute X^i. According to the insensitive microaggregation described earlier in Section 9.1, modifying one record in the data set will induce a change of at most one value in the set $S(X^i)$ of values of X^i in a cluster. Considering that marginality measures the sum of distances between a centroid candidate and all the elements in $S(X^i)$, in the worst case, in which all values in $S(X^i)$ correspond to the same boundary of $Dom(X^i)$ (defined by either Equation (9.2) or Equation (9.3)), and one of these is changed to the other boundary, the sensitivity $\Delta(m(X^i))$ will correspond to the semantic distance between both boundaries.

We have that: i) to compute the probabilities in Expression (9.5), the quality criterion $-m(S(X^i), a_j^i)$ is combined with ϵ and $\Delta(m(X^i))$, and the latter two magnitudes are constant for $Dom(X^i)$; ii) $|S(X^i)| \geq k$; iii) $m(S(X^i), a_j^i)$ is a sum of, at least, $k - 1$ terms. Hence, as the cluster size k grows, the marginalities $m(S(X^i), a_j^i)$ of values a_j^i in the cluster $S(X^i)$ have more degrees of freedom and hence tend to become more markedly diverse. Hence, as k grows, the probabilities computed in Expression (9.5) tend to become more markedly diverse, and the largest probability (the one of the optimum centroid candidate) can be expected to dominate more clearly; note that probabilities computed with Expression (9.5) decrease exponentially as marginality grows. Therefore, optimum centroids are more likely to be selected as k increases. In other words, the amount of uncertainty added to the output to fulfill differential privacy for categorical attributes decreases as the k-anonymity level of the input data increases.   □

9.5   A SEMANTIC DISTANCE FOR DIFFERENTIAL PRIVACY

As described above, the selection of differentially private outputs for categorical attributes is based on the marginality value of centroid candidates that, in turn, is a function of the semantic distance between centroids and clustered values. Moreover, the total order used to create clusters also relies on the assessment of semantic distances between attribute values. Hence, the particular measure used to compute semantic distances directly influences the quality of anonymized outputs.

A semantic distance $\delta : o \times o \rightarrow \mathbb{R}$ is a function mapping a pair of concepts to a real number that quantifies the difference between the concept meanings. A well-suited δ to achieve semantic-preserving differentially private outputs should have the following features. First, it should capture and quantify the semantics of the categorical values precisely, so that they can be well differentiated, both when defining the total order and also when selecting cluster centroids [57]. Second, from the perspective of differential privacy, δ should have a low numerical sensitivity to outlying values, that is, those that are the most distant to the rest of data. In this manner, the sensitivity of the quality criterion, which is the semantic distance of the two most outlying values of the domain, will also be low. This will produce less noisy and, hence, more accurate differentially private outputs.

The accuracy of a semantic measure depends on the kinds of techniques and knowledge bases used to perform the semantic assessments [84]. Among those relying on taxonomies, feature-based measures and measures based on intrinsic information-theoretic models usually achieve the highest accuracy with regard to human judgments of semantic distance [84]. The former measures quantify the distance between concept pairs according to their number of common and non-common taxonomic ancestors. The latter measures evaluate the similarity between concept pairs according to their mutual information, which is approximated as the number of taxonomic specializations of their most specific common ancestor. Both approaches exploit more taxonomic knowledge and, hence, tend to produce more accurate results, than well-known edge-counting measures, which quantify the distance between concepts by counting the number of taxonomic edges separating them.

On the other hand, the sensitivity to outlying values depends on the way in which semantic evidence is quantified. Many classical methods [73, 106] propose distance functions that are linearly proportional to the amount of semantic evidence observed in the taxonomy (e.g., number of taxonomic links). As a result, distances associated with outlying concepts are significantly larger than those between other more "central" values. This leads to a centroid quality criterion with a relatively high sensitivity, which negatively affects the accuracy of the Exponential Mechanism [62]. More recent methods [18, 72, 84] choose to evaluate distances in a non-linear way. Non-linear functions provide more flexibility since they can implicitly weight the contribution of more specific or more detailed concepts. As a result, concept pairs become better differentiated and semantic assessments tend to be more accurate [84]. We can distinguish between measures that exponentially promote semantic differences [18, 53] and those that aggregate semantic similarities [72, 81, 82] and differences [84] in a logarithmic way. Among these, the latter one is best suited for the differential privacy scenario, since the logarithmic assessment of the semantic differences helps reduce the relative numerical distances associated with outlying concepts and, hence, to minimize the sensitivity of the quality function used in the Exponential Mechanism.

Formally, this measure computes the distance $\delta : X^i \times X^i \to \mathbb{R}$ between two categorical values a_1^i and a_2^i of attribute X^i, whose domain is modeled in the taxonomy $\tau(X^i)$, as a logarithmic function of their number of non-common taxonomic ancestors divided (for normalization) by their total number of ancestors [84]:

$$\delta(a_1^i, a_2^i) = \log_2 \left(1 + \frac{|\phi(a_1^i) \cup \phi(a_2^i)| - |\phi(a_1^i) \cap \phi(a_2^i)|}{|\phi(a_1^i) \cup \phi(a_2^i)|} \right) \tag{9.6}$$

where $\phi(a_j^i)$ is the set of taxonomic ancestors of a_j^i in $\tau(X^i)$, including itself.

As demonstrated in [84] and [10], Expression (9.6) satisfies *non-negativity*, *reflexivity*, *symmetry*, and *subadditivity*, thereby being a distance measure in the mathematical sense.

Moreover, thanks to the normalizing denominator, the above distance is insensitive to the size and granularity of the background taxonomy, and it yields positive normalized values in the $[0, 1]$ range. Since the distance $d : Dom(X) \times Dom(X) \to \mathbb{R}$ defined in Section 9.4 is the composition of semantic distances for individual attributes and their domains may be modeled in different taxonomies, a normalized output is desirable to coherently integrate distances computed from different sources.

9.6   INTEGRATING HETEROGENEOUS ATTRIBUTE TYPES

The above-described semantic measure provides a numerical assessment of the distance between categorical attributes. As a result, given a data set X with attributes of heterogeneous data types (i.e., numerical and categorical), the record distance $d : Dom(X) \times Dom(X) \to \mathbb{R}$ required for microaggregation can be defined by composing numerically assessed distances for individual attributes, as follows:

$$d(\mathbf{x}_1, \mathbf{x}_2) = \sqrt{\frac{(dist(a_1^1, a_2^1))^2}{(dist(a_b^1, a_t^1))^2} + \cdots + \frac{(dist(a_1^m, a_2^m))^2}{(dist(a_b^m, a_t^m))^2}} \tag{9.7}$$

where $dist(a_1^i, a_2^i)$ is the distance (either numerical or semantic) between the values for the i-th attribute X^i in $\mathbf{x}_1$ and $\mathbf{x}_2$, and $dist(a_b^i, a_t^i)$ is the distance between the boundaries of $Dom(X^i)$, which is used to eliminate the influence of the attribute scale.

It can be noticed that Expression (9.7) is similar to the normalized Euclidean distance, but replacing attribute variances, which depend on input data, by distances between domain boundaries, which are insensitive to changes of input values. In this manner, the record distance function effectively defines a total order that fulfills differential privacy.

9.7   SUMMARY

This chapter has presented a method to generate differentially private data sets based on multivariate microaggregation. Following the perturbative masking approach, the protected data set can be generated by collating differentially private responses to the queries that ask for the contents of each of the records. However, since differential privacy aims at hiding the effect of any individual on the query responses, the expected accuracy of such responses is very low. Reducing the sensitivity of queries is a way to reduce the amount of noise that needs to be added to satisfy differential privacy. The method presented in this chapter operates this sensitivity reduction by using a prior multivariate microaggregation step. As a result of this step, the original records are clustered and the records in each cluster are replaced by the cluster centroid. Since each centroid depends on k records, queries on the microaggregated data set are far less sensitive to the presence or absence of any original record than queries on the original data set. Hence, much less noise needs to be added to the microaggregated data set than to the original data set to attain differential privacy; in fact, unless k is very large, the noise reduction more than compensates the distortion introduced by microaggregation.

A technical issue is that a special type of multivariate microaggregation is needed to operate the above sensitivity reduction, which we call insensitive microaggregation. Beyond defining the concept of insensitive microaggregation, we give algorithms to perform it on numerical and categorical attributes.

CHAPTER 10

Differential Privacy by Individual Ranking Microaggregation

This chapter is a follow-up of the previous one on creating differentially private data sets via perturbative masking. The previous chapter used multivariate microaggregation to reduce the sensitivity (and, thus, the required amount of noise) in the masked records. Using multivariate microaggregation to reduce the sensitivity was complex because the change of a single record in a data set could lead to multiple changes in the microaggregation clusters. We solved this issue by restricting to a class of microaggregation techniques that we called insensitive microaggregation. Moreover, the fact that a microaggregation parameter k is required that depends on the number of records n of the input data set may be problematic for large data sets. In other words, for large data sets, the required k may be so large that the utility loss incurred in the prior microaggregation step cancels the utility gain due to subsequent noise reduction. To circumvent this problem, the method described in this chapter uses univariate microaggregation instead of its multivariate counterpart. As a result, utility gains with respect to standard differential privacy are obtained regardless of the number of records of the input data set [85, 86]. In fact, using univariate microaggregation has two main advantages over multivariate microaggregation: it is simpler and it yields a sensitivity that does not depend on the size of the data set anymore (only on the number of attributes to be protected). This behavior is especially desirable in at least the following cases: i) data sets with a large number of records; ii) data sets with a small number of attributes; iii) data sets in which only the confidential attributes, which usually represent a small fraction of the total attributes, need to be protected.

10.1 LIMITATIONS OF MULTIVARIATE MICROAGGREGATION

When using insensitive multivariate microaggregation, the sensitivity of the set of n/k centroids thus obtained is $n/k \times \Delta(X)/k$ because, in the worst case.

- Changing a single record in the input data set can cause all n/k clusters to change by one record

- The record changed within each cluster can alter the value of the cluster centroid by up to $\Delta(X)/k$, where $\Delta(X)$ is the maximum distance between elements in the domain of the input data (we are assuming that centroids are computed as the arithmetic average of record values in the cluster).

The above worst-case scenario overestimates the actual sensitivity of the output and, thus, the noise to be added to the centroids to achieve ϵ-differential privacy. Indeed, it is highly unlikely that modifying one input record by up to $\Delta(X)$ would change by $\Delta(X)$ one record in *each* cluster. Let us consider an extreme scenario, in which all records in the input data set take the *maximum* possible value tuple in the domain of X. Recall that the insensitive microaggregation used sorts and groups records according to a total order defined over the domain of X. Then, assume that the record located in the last position of the sorted list changes to take the *minimum* value tuple of the domain of X, so that its distance to any of the other records in the data set is $\Delta(X)$. According to the ordering criterion, such a change would cause the modified record to be "inserted" in the first position of the sorted list. Consequently, all other records would be moved to the next position, which would change *all* clusters by one record. However, from the perspective of the centroid computation (i.e., the average of the record in the group), only the first cluster centroid, where the modified record is located, would change and its variation would be exactly $\Delta(X)/k$.

In other intermediate scenarios, the effect of modifying one record would be split among the centroids of the clusters affected by the modification. Intuitively, the aggregation of the centroid variations would seem to be upper-bounded by $\Delta(X)/k$, which corresponds to the extreme case detailed above. However, this is only true if a total order for the domain of X exists for which the triangular inequality is satisfied, that is, when $d(r_1, r_2) + d(r_2, r_3) \geq d(r_1, r_3)$ holds for any records r_1, r_2, and r_3 in X. Unfortunately, this is generally not the case for multivariate data because a natural total order does not always exist. Artificial total orders defined for multivariate data do not fulfill the triangular inequality and, as discussed above, the sensitivity of individual centroids should be multiplied by the number of released centroids ($n/k \times \Delta(X)/k$) to satisfy differential privacy.

The lack of a total order does not occur in univariate numerical data sets, that is, those with just one attribute. With a single numerical attribute, a natural total order (the usual numerical order) can be easily defined with respect to the minimum or maximum value of the domain of values of the attribute so that the triangular inequality is fulfilled. In these conditions, it is shown in [21] that clusters in the optimal microaggregation partition contain consecutive values. The next lemma shows that the sensitivity of the set of centroids is indeed $\Delta(X)/k$.

Lemma 10.1   Let $x_1, \cdots, x_n$ be a totally ordered set of values that has been microaggregated into $\lfloor n/k \rfloor$ clusters of k consecutive values each, except perhaps one cluster that contains up to $2k - 1$ consecutive values. Let the centroids of these clusters be $\bar{x}_1, \cdots, \bar{x}_{\lfloor n/k \rfloor}$, respectively. Now if, for any single i, x_i is replaced by x_i' such that $|x_i' - x_i| \leq \Delta$ and new clusters and centroids

$\bar{x}'_1, \cdots, \bar{x}'_{\lfloor n/k \rfloor}$ are computed, it holds that

$$\sum_{j=1}^{\lfloor n/k \rfloor} |\bar{x}'_j - \bar{x}_j| \leq \Delta/k.$$

Proof. Assume without loss of generality that $x'_i > x_i$ (the proof for $x'_i < x_i$ is symmetric). Assume, for the sake of simplicity, that n is a multiple of k (we will later relax this assumption). Hence, exactly n/k clusters are obtained, with cluster j containing consecutive values from $x_{(j-1)k+1}$ to x_{jk}. Let j_i be the cluster to which x_i belongs. We can distinguish two cases, namely $x'_i \leq x_{j_i k+1}$ and $x'_i > x_{j_i k+1}$.

Case 1. When $x'_i \leq x_{j_i k+1}$, x'_i stays in j_i. Thus, the centroids of all clusters other than j_i stay unchanged and the centroid of cluster j_i increases by Δ/k, because $x'_i = x_i + \Delta$. So the lemma follows in this case.

Case 2. When $x'_i > x_{j_i k+1}$, two or more clusters change as a result of replacing x_i by x'_i: cluster j_i loses x_i and another cluster j'_i (for $j'_i > j_i$) acquires x'_i. To maintain its cardinality k, after losing x_i, cluster j_i acquires $x_{j_i k+1}$. In turn, cluster $j_i + 1$ loses $x_{j_i k+1}$ and acquires $x_{(j_i+1)k+1}$, and so on, until cluster j'_i, which transfers its smallest value $x_{(j'_i-1)k+1}$ to cluster $j'_i - 1$ and acquires x'_i. From cluster $j'_i + 1$ upward, nothing changes. Hence the overall impact on centroids is

$$\sum_{j=1}^{n/k} |\bar{x}'_j - \bar{x}_j| = \sum_{j=j_i}^{j'_i} |\bar{x}'_j - \bar{x}_j|$$

$$= \frac{x_{j_i k+1} - x_i}{k} + \frac{x_{(j_i+1)k+1} - x_{j_i k+1}}{k} + \cdots + \frac{x'_i - x_{(j'_i-1)k+1}}{k}$$

$$= \frac{x'_i - x_i}{k} = \frac{\Delta}{k}. \tag{10.1}$$

Hence, the lemma follows also in this case.

Now consider the general situation in which n is not a multiple of k. In this situation there are $\lfloor n/k \rfloor$ clusters and one of them contains between $k + 1$ and $2k - 1$ values. If we are in Case 1 above and this larger cluster is cluster j_i, the centroid of j_i changes by less than Δ/k, so the lemma also holds; of course if the larger cluster is one of the other clusters, it is unaffected and the lemma also holds. If we are in Case 2 above and the larger cluster is one the clusters that change, one of the fractions in the third term of Expression (10.1) above has a denominator greater than k and hence the overall sum is less than Δ/k, so the lemma also holds; if the larger cluster is one of the unaffected ones, the lemma also holds. □

10.2 SENSITIVITY REDUCTION VIA INDIVIDUAL RANKING

From the previous section, it turns out that, for univariate data sets, the amount of noise needed to fulfill differential privacy after the microaggregation step is significantly lower than with the multivariate insensitive microaggregation method in Chapter 9 (i.e., $\Delta(X)/k$ vs. $n/k \times \Delta(X)/k$). Moreover, this noise is exactly $1/k$-th of the noise required by the standard differential privacy approach, in which the sensitivity is $\Delta(X)$ because *any* output record may change by $\Delta(X)$ following a modification of any record in the input.

To benefit from such a noise reduction in the case of multivariate data sets, we rely on the sequential composition property of differential privacy (see Section 8.1). As discussed in Section 9.1, in the context of differentially private data publishing, we can think of a data release as the collected answers to successive queries for each record in the data set. Let $I_r(X)$ be the query that returns the value of record r (from a total of n records) in the data set X. In turn, we can think of $I_r(X)$ as the collected answers to successive queries for each of the attributes of record r. Let $I_{ra}(X)$ be the query function that returns the value of attribute a (from a total of m attributes). We have $I_r(X) = (I_{r1}(X), \ldots, I_{rm}(X))$. The differentially private data set that we seek can be generated by giving a differentially private answer to the set of queries $I_{ra}(X)$ for all $r = 1, \ldots, n$ and all $a = 1, \ldots, m$. Differential privacy being designed to protect the privacy of individuals, such queries are very sensitive and require a large amount of noise.

To reduce sensitivity and hence the amount of noise needed to attain differential privacy, we rely on individual ranking microaggregation; as discussed in Section 3.2, individual ranking is more utility-preserving than multivariate microaggregation. Rather than querying for $I_{ra}(X)$, the data set is generated by querying for individual ranking microaggregation centroids. Let $\rho_X(r, a)$ be the group of records of data set X in the individual ranking microaggregation of attribute a that corresponds to r, and let $C_{\rho_X(r,a)}$ be the associated centroid. We replace $I_{ra}(X)$ by $C_{\rho_X(r,a)}$.

Now, we have to minimize the amount of noise required to answer these queries in a differentially private manner. We work with each attribute independently and then combine the queries corresponding to different attributes by applying sequential composition. If we get an ϵ-differentially private response to $(C_{\rho_X(1,a)}, \ldots, C_{\rho_X(n,a)})$ for each $a = 1, \ldots, m$, then by joining them we have $m\epsilon$-differential privacy.

For attribute a, we have to answer the query $(C_{\rho_X(1,a)}, \ldots, C_{\rho_X(n,a)})$ in an ϵ-differentially private manner. If we compute the L_1-sensitivity of this query, s_a, we can attain ϵ-differential privacy by adding a Laplace distributed noise with scale parameter s_a/ϵ to each component $C_{\rho_X(i,a)}$. We have already seen that for individual ranking microaggregation the L_1-sensitivity of the list of centroids is Δ_a/k. However, in our query each centroid appears k (or more times); hence, the sensitivity is multiplied by k and becomes Δ_a (or greater), which is not satisfactory. Our goal is to show that we can attain ϵ-differential privacy by adding a Laplace noise with scale $\Delta_a/(k\epsilon)$ rather than Δ_a/ϵ (as an L_1-sensitivity of Δ_a would require). To that end, instead of taking an independent draw of the noise distribution for each of the components, we use the same draw for all the components that refer to the same centroid. That is, we use the same random variable

$L_{\rho X(r,a)}$ to determine the amount of noise that is added to all the components sharing the same value $C_{\rho X(r,a)}$; similarly, in data set X' we use $L_{\rho X'(r,a)}$ as noise for all components sharing the same value $C_{\rho X'(r,a)}$. For ϵ-differential privacy, it must hold that

$$\frac{\Pr((C_{\rho X(1,a)} + L_{\rho X(1,a)}, \ldots, C_{\rho X(n,a)} + L_{\rho X(n,a)}) = (x_1, \ldots, x_n))}{\Pr((C_{\rho X'(1,a)} + L_{\rho X'(1,a)}, \ldots, C_{\rho X'(n,a)} + L_{\rho X'(n,a)}) = (x_1, \ldots, x_n))} \le \exp(\epsilon).$$

If any of $x_1, \ldots, x_n$ is not a centroid value plus the noise corresponding to that centroid value (note that equal centroid values are added equal noise values, as said above), the probabilities in both the numerator and the denominator of the above expression are zero, and differential privacy is satisfied. Otherwise, we have that $x_1, \ldots, x_n$ are only repetitions of n/k different values, that is, the values of the n/k centroids plus the noise corresponding to each centroid value. Thus, we can simplify the expression by removing all but one of each of those repetitions. Let $C_{i,a}(X)$ and $C_{i,a}(X')$ for $i = 1, \ldots, n/k$ be the centroid values for attribute a associated to X and X', respectively, and $L_{i,a}$ and $L'_{i,a}$ be Laplace noises with scale $\Delta_a/(k\epsilon)$ associated with those centroid values, respectively. After rewriting the above inequality in these terms and taking into account that the sensitivity of the list of centroids is Δ_a/k, it is evident that ϵ-differential privacy is satisfied.

$$\frac{\Pr((C_{1,a}(X) + L_{1,a}, \ldots, C_{n/k,a}(X) + L_{n/k,a}) = (x'_1, \ldots, x'_{n/k}))}{\Pr((C_{1,a}(X') + L'_{1,a}, \ldots, C_{n/k,a}(X') + L'_{n/k,a}) = (x'_1, \ldots, x'_{n/k}))} \le \exp(\epsilon).$$

Hence, we propose Algorithm 10 to obtain a differentially private version X^D of a numerical original data set X with attributes $X^1, \ldots, X^m$.

Algorithm 10 Generation of a ϵ-differentially private data set via individual-ranking microaggregation for numerical attributes

---

1. Use individual-ranking microaggregation independently on each attribute X^i, for $i = 1$ to m.

2. Within each cluster, replace *all* attribute values by the cluster centroid value, so that each microaggregated cluster consists of k repeated centroid values. Let the resulting microaggregated data set be $\bar{X}$.

3. Add Laplace noise independently to each attribute $\bar{X}^i$ of $\bar{X}$, where the scale parameter for attribute $\bar{X}^i$ is

$$\Delta(\bar{X}^i)/\epsilon = \Delta(X^i)/(k \times \epsilon).$$

The *same* noise perturbation is used on all repeated centroid values within each cluster.

Now we can state the following.

Lemma 10.2   The data set output by Algorithm 10 is $m\epsilon$-differentially private.

Proof. The lemma follows from the previous discussion in this section.   □

Note. In Step 3 of Algorithm 10, it is critically important to add exactly the same noise perturbation to all repeated values within a microaggregated cluster. If we used different random perturbations for each repeated value, the resulting noise-added cluster would be equivalent to the answers to k independent queries. This would multiply by k the sensitivity of the centroid, which would cancel the sensitivity reduction brought by microaggregation in Step 1.

10.3   CHOOSING THE MICROGGREGATION PARAMETER k

In order to obtain an ϵ-differentially private data set, by parallel composition it suffices to make each record ϵ-differentially private. In turn, to make a record ϵ-differentially private, we have two possibilities.

1. *Plain Laplace noise addition without microaggregation.* Given that each record has m attributes, by sequential composition we need (ϵ/m)-differentially private attribute values to obtain an ϵ-differentially private record. Hence, Laplace noise addition with scale parameter $\Delta(X^i)/(\epsilon/m) = m\Delta(X^i)/\epsilon$ needs to be added to each attribute X^i.

2. *Laplace noise addition with individual ranking microaggregation.* When performing individual-ranking microaggregation and replacing original values by cluster centroids, we preserve the structure of records. By sequential composition, to make a record of $\bar{X}$ ϵ-differentially private, we need to make attributes in $\bar{X}$ (ϵ/m)-differentially private. Hence, Laplace noise addition with scale parameter $\Delta(\bar{X}^i)/(\epsilon/m) = m\Delta(\bar{X}^i)/\epsilon$ needs to be added to each attribute $\bar{X}^i$. However, dealing with $\bar{X}^i$ rather than X^i is better, because $\bar{X}^i$ is less sensitive. Indeed, $\Delta(\bar{X}^i) = \Delta(X^i)/k$, so the scale parameter is $m\Delta(\bar{X}^i)/(k\epsilon)$.

According to the above discussion, our approach adds less noise than plain Laplace noise addition for any $k > 1$. Admittedly, its prior individual ranking microaggregation causes some additional information loss. However, this information loss grows very slowly with the cluster size k and also with the number of attributes m, whereas the Laplace noise being added decreases very quickly with k.

10.4   SUMMARY

Like the previous chapter, this chapter has presented a method to generate a differentially private data set based on microaggregation. Rather than multivariate microaggregation, univariate microaggregation has been used. Univariate microaggregation enables further reduction of the noise scale parameter in most scenarios, which is of utmost importance for data analysis. The method described in this chapter is also easier to implement, because the individual ranking algorithm only relies on the natural order of individual attributes. Moreover, for n records and

m attributes, its computational cost is $O(n \times m)$, whereas insensitive multivariate microaggregation takes $O(n \times n)$. Since usually $n \gg m$, the current method is more scalable as the number of records in a data set grows. Finally, prior individual-ranking microaggregation incurs less information loss than prior multivariate microaggregation. Even though the discussion was focused on numerical attributes, by using the alternative mechanisms introduced in Section 9.4, the method detailed here can also be applied to categorical data.

C H A P T E R   11

Conclusions and Research Directions

In this book, we have offered a comprehensive overview of privacy threats and protection mechanisms for microdata releases, which focus on identity and/or attribute disclosure. These are tightly related to the two views of privacy that have been presented in Chapter 2: anonymity (it should not be possible to re-identify any individual in the published data) and confidentiality or secrecy (access to the released data should not reveal confidential information related to any specific individual).

11.1 SUMMARY AND CONCLUSIONS

We have seen that statistical disclosure control for microdata is attained through data modification (by either masking the original data set or replacing it with a synthetic data set). The protected (modified) version of the original data set is then released while the original data set is kept private. The modifications operated on the data during the SDC process damage their utility. The goal in SDC should be to modify data in such a way that sufficient protection is provided at minimum utility loss. However, measuring utility is a complex topic. The main difficulty is that utility depends not only on the modifications performed on the data but also on the intended data uses. Since potential data uses are very diverse and it may even be hard to identify them all at the moment of the data release, microdata protection can seldom be performed in a data use-specific manner. Thus, it is usually more appropriate to refer to information loss rather than to utility. Measures of information loss provide generic ways for the data protector to assess how much harm is being inflicted to the data by a particular masking technique.

There is a large body of methods for disclosure control of microdata (see Chapter 3). These methods can be applied to obtain *ex post* or *ex ante* privacy. The *ex post* approach is the usual one in the statistical community, and it prioritizes publishing analytically valid data; disclosure risk is measured after the data have been protected and, in case it is considered too high, more stringent privacy parameters or even a different SDC method are used to bring the risk down to an acceptable level. The *ex ante* approach is mainly advocated in the computer science community, and it focuses on guaranteeing from the outset that the disclosure risk is below a specified level; this is done via a privacy model and no utility considerations are taken into account.

Privacy models state the conditions to be satisfied by the protected data for disclosure risk to be under control. However, they do not specify the SDC method to be employed to attain these conditions. Among the privacy models we have reviewed, k-anonymity and its derivatives can be classified as syntactic privacy models: they determine the form that the protected data set must have to limit disclosure risk. This form is usually determined by making assumptions about the information available to intruders and the approach that the latter will follow in an attack. For instance, in k-anonymity is it assumed that intruders proceed by linking the quasi-identifier attributes to an external non-anonymous data set. Thus, by requiring each combination of quasi-identifier values to be shared by at least k records in the protected data set, accurate re-identification is prevented. Unlike syntactic privacy models, differential privacy specifies conditions on the data generation process rather than on the generated data.

k-anonymity-like models and differential privacy take completely different approaches to disclosure limitation. However, we have shown in Chapter 8 that, if the assumptions about the intruder made in t-closeness are satisfied, the protection offered by t-closeness and the protection offered by differential privacy are equivalent.

We have also demonstrated that, beyond being a family of SDC methods, microaggregation is a useful primitive to find bridges between privacy models. While attaining k-anonymity through microaggregation is rather intuitive, we have also described several more elaborate approaches to attain t-closeness based on microaggregation (see Chapter 7). When generating differentially private data sets via perturbative masking, microaggregation has also been used to reduce data sensitivity and, thus, the amount of noise addition required to fulfill differential privacy. An approach based on a special type of multivariate k-anonymous microaggregation, called insensitive microaggregation, has been described in Chapter 9, whereas a method based on univariate microaggregation that offers better utility for large data sets has been described in Chapter 10.

11.2   RESEARCH DIRECTIONS

In addition to the conventional data release scenarios considered in this book, the current research agenda in data privacy includes more challenging settings that require further research.

On the one hand, the (legitimate) ambition to leverage *big data* by releasing them poses several problems [13, 55, 93]. In the conventional data protection scenario, the data set is of moderate size, it comes from a single source and it is static (it is a snapshot). Hence, it can be protected independently from other data sets by the data collector. In contrast, big data are often created by gathering and merging heterogeneous data from different sources, which may already have been anonymized by the sources. To further complicate matters, these sources may be dynamic, that is, they may provide continuous data streams (e.g., sensor readings that keep flowing in over time). Thus, the data protector faces the following challenges.

- *Scalability*. The sheer volume of big data sets can render many of the available protection methods impractical. The *computational cost* of the algorithms employed for anonymization should be carefully pondered.

- *Linkability*. If merging sensitive data from several sources, the incoming data may already have been anonymized at the source (in fact they probably should). Hence, the ability to link anonymized records from several sources that correspond to the same individual is a crucial issue. At the same time, the requirement to preserve some amount of linkability may restrict the range of eligible anonymization methods.

- *Composability*. A privacy model is composable if the privacy guarantees it offers are totally or partially preserved after repeated independent applications of the model. Clearly, when aggregating anonymized data from several sources, composability is fundamental if the aggregated data have to offer some privacy guarantee.

- *Dynamicity*. Data may be continuous, transient, and even unbounded. It may be hard to enforce the usual privacy models in this situation. Furthermore, there is a need to minimize the delay between the incoming data and the corresponding anonymized output [11] and, thus, protection algorithms should be efficient enough to be run in real time or quasi-real time.

Also partly related to the explosion of big data, there is an increasing social and political pressure to empower the citizens regarding their own data. Specifically, the forthcoming European Union's General Data Protection Regulation [5] makes significant steps in this direction. As a consequence, transparency, intervenability, and even self-anonymization become very relevant technical requirements [13]. Privacy-preserving technologies are needed that empower the data subjects to understand, check, control, and even perform themselves the protection of their data. In this respect, local anonymization [89] (whereby subjects locally anonymize their data so that they can be later merged with other subjects' data to form a data set that still satisfies a certain privacy model) or collaborative anonymization [94] (whereby subjects collaborate to anonymize their respective data so that they get as much privacy as with local anonymization and as little information loss as with centralized anonymization) are promising approaches.

Finally, as pointed out in [15], privacy by design (for which anonymization and statistical disclosure control are tools) cannot protect all individual rights related to data. Very connected to the right to privacy is the right to non-discrimination. When automated decisions are made based on inference rules learned by data mining algorithms from training data biased w.r.t. discriminatory (sensitive) attributes like gender, ethnicity, religion, etc., discriminatory decisions may ensue. As a result, individuals may be unfairly deprived of rights and benefits they are entitled to. Even if the training data contain no sensitive attributes, these may be inferred by the data mining algorithms based on other attributes (e.g., in some cases the ethnicity can be guessed from the place of residence, or the gender from the job, etc.) which may still allow indirect discrimination. Detection of discrimination in data mining was first introduced in [71]. Sanitization methods for training data to prevent direct or indirect discrimination were proposed in [37, 39]. In [38, 40] it was shown that synergies can be found between sanitization for anti-discrimination and sanitization for privacy preservation: if adequately done, sanitizing for one purpose may go a long way toward sanitizing for the other purpose, which allows attaining both goals with less information loss than if pursuing them independently.

The need for anti-discrimination becomes even more pressing in the time of big data analytics. As warned in [13], analytics applied to combined data sets aim at building specific profiles for individuals that can be used in the context of automated decision making systems, that is, to include or exclude individuals from specific offers, services, or products. Such profiling can in certain cases lead to isolation and/or discrimination, including price differentiation, credit denial, exclusion from jobs or benefits, etc., without providing the individuals with the possibility to contest these decisions. Extending the above-mentioned synergies between anti-discrimination and privacy preservation to big data coming from several sources is a worthy research endeavor requiring further work.

Bibliography

[1] Directive 95/46/ec of the european parliament and of the council of 24 october 1995 on the protection of individuals with regard to the processing of personal data and on the free movement of such data. *Official Journal of the European Communities*, pages 31–50, October 1995. 4

[2] Standard for privacy of individually identifiable health information. *Federal Register, Special Edition*, pages 768–769, October 2007. 4

[3] Timeline: a history of privacy in america, 1600-2008. *Scientific American*, 2008. 4

[4] Timeline: privacy and the law. *NPR*, 2009. 4

[5] General Data Protection Regulation. Technical report, European Union, 2015. 107

[6] C.C. Aggarwal. On k-anonymity and the curse of dimensionality. In *Proceedings of the 31st International Conference on Very Large Data Bases*, pages 901–909, 2005. 44

[7] M. Barbaro and T. Zeller. A face is exposed for AOL searcher no. 4417749. *The New York Times*, August 2006. 32

[8] M. Batet, A. Erola, D. Sánchez, and J. Castellà. Utility preserving query log anonymization via semantic microaggregation. *Information Sciences*, 242:49–63, 2013. DOI: 10.1016/j.ins.2013.04.020. 56

[9] M. Batet, A. Erola, D. Sánchez, and Castellá-Roca. Semantic anonymisation of set-valued data. In *Proceedings of the 6th International Conference on Agents and Artificial Intelligence*, volume 1, pages 102–112, Lisbon, Portugal, 2014. 21

[10] M. Batet, A. Valls, and K. Gibert. A distance function to assess the similarity of words using ontologies. In *XV Congreso Español sobre Tecnologías y Lógica Fuzzy*, pages 561–566, Huelva, Spain, 2010. 94

[11] J. Cao, B. Carminati, E. Ferrari, and K.-L. Tan. Castle: continuously anonymizing data streams. *IEEE Transactions on Dep*, 8(3):337–352, 2011. DOI: 10.1109/TDSC.2009.47. 107

[12] G. Cormode, C. Procopiuc, D. Srivastava, E. Shen, and T. Yu. Differentially private spatial decompositions. In *Proceedings of the 28th IEEE International Conference on Data*

Engineering, ICDE '12, pages 20–31, Washington, DC, 2012. IEEE Computer Society. DOI: 10.1109/ICDE.2012.16. 76

[13] G. D'Acquisto, J. Domingo-Ferrer, P. Kikiras, V. Torra, Y.-A. de Montjoye, and A. Bourka. Privacy by design in big data – an overview of privacy enhancing technologies in the era of big data analytics. Technical report, European Union Agency for Network and Information Security, 2015. DOI: 10.2824/641480. 106, 107, 108

[14] T. Dalenius. Towards a methodology for statistical disclosure control. *Statistik Tidskrift*, 15:429–444, 1977. 6

[15] G. Danezis, J. Domingo-Ferrer, M. Hansen, J.-H. Hoepman, D. Le Métayer, R. Tirtea, and S. Schiffner. Privacy and data protection by design – from policy to engineering. Technical report, European Union Agency for Network and Information Security, 2015. 107

[16] D. Defays and M.N. Anwar. Masking microdata using micro-aggregation. *Journal of Official Statistics*, 14(4):449–461, 1998. 20

[17] D. Defays and P. Nanopoulos. Panels of enterprises and confidentiality: the small aggregates method. In *Proceedings of 92 Symposium on Design and Analysis of Longitudinal Surveys*, pages 195–204, Ottawa, Canada, 1993. 20

[18] J. Domingo-Ferrer. Marginality: a numerical mapping for enhanced exploitation of taxonomic attributes. In V. Torra, Y. Narukawa, B. López, and M. Villaret, editors, *MDAI*, volume 7647 of *Lecture Notes in Computer Science*, pages 367–381. Springer, 2012. 93

[19] J. Domingo-Ferrer and U. González-Nicolás. Hybrid microdata using microaggregation. *Information Sciences*, 180(15):2384–2844, 2010. DOI: 10.1016/j.ins.2010.04.005. 10, 21

[20] J. Domingo-Ferrer, A. Martínez-Ballesté, J. M. Mateo-Sanz, and F. Sebé. Efficient multivariate data-oriented microaggregation. *The VLDB Journal*, 15(4):355–369, November 2006. DOI: 10.1007/s00778-006-0007-0. 20

[21] J. Domingo-Ferrer and J. M. Mateo-Sanz. Practical data-oriented microaggregation for statistical disclosure control. *IEEE Transactions on Knowledge and Data Engineering*, 14(1):189–201, 2002. DOI: 10.1109/69.979982. 20, 98

[22] J. Domingo-Ferrer, J. M. Mateo-Sanz, A. Oganian, V. Torra, and A. Torres. On the security of microaggregation with individual ranking: analytical attacks. *International Journal of Uncertainty, Fuzziness and Knowledge-Based Systems*, 18(5):477–492, 2002. DOI: 10.1142/S0218488502001594. 20

[23] J. Domingo-Ferrer, D. Sánchez, and G. Rufian-Torrell.   Anonymization of nominal data based on semantic marginality. *Information Sciences*, 242:35–48, 2013. DOI: 10.1016/j.ins.2013.04.021. 11, 56, 89, 90

[24] J. Domingo-Ferrer and J. Soria-Comas.   From t-closeness to differential privacy and vice versa in data anonymization. *Knowledge-Based Systems*, 74:151–158, 2015. DOI: 10.1016/j.knosys.2014.11.011. 73, 75

[25] J. Domingo-Ferrer and V. Torra. A quantitative comparison of disclosure control methods for microdata. In P. Doyle, J.I. Lane, J.J.M. Theeuwes, and L. Zayatz, editors, *Confidentiality, Disclosure and Data Access: Theory and Practical Applications for Statistical Agencies*, pages 111–134. North-Holland, Amsterdam, 2001. 11, 12, 13, 20

[26] J. Domingo-Ferrer and V. Torra.   Ordinal, continuous and heterogeneous k-anonymity through microaggregation. *Data Mining and Knowledge Discovery*, 11(2):195–212, 2005. DOI: 10.1007/s10618-005-0007-5. 20, 42, 54, 90

[27] J. Drechsler. *Synthetic datasets for statistical disclosure control*, volume 201 of *Lecture Notes in Statistics*. Springer-Verlag New York, 2011. DOI: 10.1007/978-1-4614-0326-5. 9, 22

[28] G.T. Duncan, S.E. Fienberg, R. Krishnan, R. Padman, and S.F. Roehrig.   Disclosure limitation methods and information loss for tabular data. In *Confidentiality, Disclosure and Data Access: Theory and Practical Applications for Statistical Agencies*, pages 135–166. North-Holland, Amsterdam, North-Holland, 2001. 13

[29] C. Dwork. Differential privacy. In M. Bugliesi, B. Preneel, V. Sassone, and I. Wegener, editors, *Automata, Languages and Programming*, volume 4052 of *Lecture Notes in Computer Science*, pages 1–12. Springer Berlin/Heidelberg, 2006. DOI: 10.1007/11787006. 6, 18, 65

[30] C. Dwork, G.N. Rothblum, and S. Vadhan.   Boosting and differential privacy. In *51st Annual IEEE Symposium on Foundations of Computer Science (FOCS)*, pages 51–60, Oct 2010. DOI: 10.1109/FOCS.2010.12. 66

[31] H. Feistel.   Cryptography and computer privacy. *Scientific American*, 228:15–23, 1973. DOI: 10.1038/scientificamerican0573-15. 3

[32] I. P. Fellegi and A. B. Sunter. A theory for record linkage. *Journal of the American Statistical Association*, 64:1183–1210, 1969. DOI: 10.1080/01621459.1969.10501049. 27, 28

[33] A. Ghosh, T. Roughgarden, and M. Sundararajan.   Universally utility-maximizing privacy mechanisms. In M. Mitzenmacher, editor, *STOC*, pages 351–360. ACM, 2009. 18

[34] D. J. Glancy. The invention of the right to privacy. *Arizona Law Review*, 27:1–39, 1979. 3

[35] P. Golle. Revisiting the uniqueness of simple demographics in the us population. In *Proceedings of the 5th ACM Workshop on Privacy in Electronic Society*, WPES '06, pages 77–80, New York, 2006. DOI: 10.1145/1179601.1179615. 31

[36] B. Greenberg. Rank swapping for ordinal data. Washington DC: US Bureau of the Census, 1987. 18

[37] S. Hajian and J. Domingo-Ferrer. A methodology for direct and indirect discrimination prevention in data mining. *IEEE Transactions on Knowledge and Data Engineering*, 25(7):1445–1459, 2013. DOI: 10.1109/TKDE.2012.72. 107

[38] S. Hajian, J. Domingo-Ferrer, and O. Farràs. Generalization-based privacy preservation and discrimination prevention in data publishing and mining. *Data Mining and Knowledge Discovery*, 28(5-6):1158–1188, 2014. DOI: 10.1007/s10618-014-0346-1. 107

[39] S. Hajian, J. Domingo-Ferrer, and A. Martínez-Ballesté. Rule protection for indirect discrimination prevention in data mining. In *Modeling Decision for Artificial Intelligence*, volume 6820 of *Lecture Notes in Computer Science*, pages 211–222. Springer, 2011. DOI: 10.1007/978-3-642-22589-5_20. 107

[40] S. Hajian, J. Domingo-Ferrer, A. Monreale, D. Pedreschi, and F. Giannotti. Discrimination- and privacy-aware patterns. *Data Mining and Knowledge Discovery*, 29(6):1733–1782, 2015. DOI: 10.1007/s10618-014-0393-7. 107

[41] S. L. Hansen and S. Mukherjee. A polynomial algorithm for optimal univariate microaggregation. *IEEE Transactions on Knowledge and Data Engineering*, 15(4):1043–1044, 2003. DOI: 10.1109/TKDE.2003.1209020. 20

[42] M. Hay, V. Rastogi, G. Miklau, and D. Suciu. Boosting the accuracy of differentially private histograms through consistency. *Proceedings of the VLDB Endowment*, 3(1-2):1021–1032, September 2010. DOI: 10.14778/1920841.1920970. 76

[43] J. Holvast. History of privacy. In V. Matyáš, S. Fischer-Hübner, D. Cvrček, and P. Švenda, editors, *The Future of Identity in the Information Society*, volume 298 of *IFIP Advances in Information and Communication Technology*, pages 13–42. Springer Berlin Heidelberg, 2009. DOI: 10.1007/978-3-642-03315-5. 4

[44] A. Hundepool, J. Domingo-Ferrer, L. Franconi, S. Giessing, E. Schulte-Nordholt, K. Spicer, and P.P. de Wolf. *Statistical Disclosure Control*. Wiley, 2012. DOI: 10.1002/9781118348239. 8, 17

[45] A. Hundepool, A. Van de Wetering, R. Ramaswamy, L. Franconi, A. Capobianchi, P.-P. DeWolf, J. Domingo-Ferrer, V. Torra, R. Brand, and S. Giessing. *μ-ARGUS version 4.2 Software and User's Manual*. Statistics Netherlands, Voorburg NL, 2008. http://neon.vb.cbs.nl/casc. 16, 20

[46] S. Inusah and T. J. Kozubowski. A discrete analogue of the laplace distribution. *Journal of Statistical Planning and Inference*, 136(3):1090–1102, 2006. DOI: 10.1016/j.jspi.2004.08.014. 69

[47] M. A. Jaro. Advances in record-linkage methodology as applied to matching the 1985 census of tampa, florida. *Journal of the American Statistical Association*, 84(406):414–420, 1989. DOI: 10.1080/01621459.1989.10478785. 27

[48] J. J. Kim. A method for limiting disclosure in microdata based on random noise and transformation. In *Proceedings of the Section on Survey Research Methods*, pages 303–308, Alexandria VA, 1986. American Statistical Association. 17

[49] M. Laszlo and S. Mukherjee. Minimum spanning tree partitioning algorithm for microaggregation. *IEEE Transactions on Knowledge and Data Engineering*, 17(7):902–911, July 2005. DOI: 10.1109/TKDE.2005.112. 20

[50] N. Li, T. Li, and S. Venkatasubramanian. t-closeness: privacy beyond k-anonymity and l-diversity. In R. Chirkova, A. Dogac, M. T. Özsu, and T. K. Sellis, editors, *ICDE*, pages 106–115. IEEE, 2007. 48, 49, 51, 53

[51] N. Li, T. Li, and S. Venkatasubramanian. Closeness: a new privacy measure for data publishing. *IEEE Transactions on Knowledge and Data Engineering*, 22(7):943–956, July 2010. DOI: 10.1109/TKDE.2009.139. 53

[52] N. Li, W. Yang, and W. Qardaji. Differentially private grids for geospatial data. In *Proceedings of the 2013 IEEE International Conference on Data Engineering (ICDE 2013)*, ICDE '13, pages 757–768, Washington, DC, 2013. IEEE Computer Society. DOI: 10.1109/ICDE.2013.6544872. 76

[53] Y. Li, Z. A. Bandar, and D. McLean. An approach for measuring semantic similarity between words using multiple information sources. *IEEE Transactions on Knowledge and Data Engineering*, 15(4):871–882, July 2003. DOI: 10.1109/TKDE.2003.1209005. 93

[54] A. Machanavajjhala, D. Kifer, J. Gehrke, and M. Venkitasubramaniam. l-diversity: privacy beyond k-anonymity. *ACM Transactions on Knowledge Discovery from Data*, 1(1), March 2007. 47, 75

[55] A. Machanavajjhala and J. Reiter. Big privacy: protecting confidentiality in big data. *XRDS: Crossroads*, 19(1):20–23, 2012. DOI: 10.1145/2331042.2331051. 106

[56] S. Martínez, D. Sánchez, and A. Valls. Evaluation of the disclosure risk of masking methods dealing with textual attributes. *International Journal of Innovative Computing, Information and Control*, 8(7):4869–4882, 2012. DOI: 10.1016/j.inffus.2011.03.004. 26

[57] S. Martínez, D. Sánchez, and A. Valls. Semantic adaptive microaggregation of categorical microdata. *Computers & Security*, 31(5):653–672, 2012. DOI: 10.1016/j.cose.2012.04.003. 11, 20, 21, 56, 89, 90, 93

[58] S. Martínez, D. Sánchez, and A. Valls. Towards k-anonymous non-numerical data via semantic resampling. In *Proceedings of the 14th International Conference on Information Processing and Management of Uncertainty in Knowledge-Based Systems*, pages 519–528, Montpellier, France, 2012. DOI: 10.1007/978-3-642-31724-8_54. 15

[59] S. Martínez, D. Sánchez, and A. Valls. A semantic framework to protect the privacy of electronic health records with non-numerical attributes. *Journal of Biomedical Informatics*, 46(2):294–303, 2013. DOI: 10.1016/j.jbi.2012.11.005. 11

[60] S. Martínez, D. Sánchez, A. Valls, and Batet. Privacy protection of textual attributes through a semantic-based masking method. *Information Fusion*, 13(4):304–314, 2012. DOI: 10.1016/j.inffus.2011.03.004. 11

[61] J. M. Mateo-Sanz, J. Domingo-Ferrer, and F. Sebé. Probabilistic information loss measures in confidentiality protection of continuous microdata. *Data Mining and Knowledge Discovery*, 11(2):181–193, 2005. DOI: 10.1007/s10618-005-0011-9. 12

[62] F. McSherry and K. Talwar. Mechanism design via differential privacy. In *Proceedings of the 48th Annual IEEE Symposium on Foundations of Computer Science*, FOCS '07, pages 94–103, Washington, DC, 2007. IEEE Computer Society. DOI: 10.1109/FOCS.2007.41. 72, 91, 93

[63] D.J. Mir, S. Isaacman, R. Caceres, M. Martonosi, and R.N. Wright. Dp-where: differentially private modeling of human mobility. In *2013 IEEE International Conference on Big Data*, pages 580–588, Oct 2013. DOI: 10.1109/BigData.2013.6691626. 76

[64] N. Mohammed, R. Chen, B. C.M. Fung, and P. S. Yu. Differentially private data release for data mining. In *Proceedings of the 17th ACM SIGKDD International Conference on Knowledge Discovery and Data Mining*, KDD '11, pages 493–501, New York, 2011. DOI: 10.1145/2020408.2020487. 76

[65] K. Muralidhar and R. Sarathy. Generating sufficiency-based non-synthetic perturbed data. *Transactions on Data Privacy*, 1(1):17–33, 2008. 10, 21

[66] G. Navarro. A guided tour to approximate string matching. *ACM Computing Surveys*, 33(1):31–88, March 2001. DOI: 10.1145/375360.375365. 25

[67] C.L. Newman, D.J. Blake, and C.J. Merz. UCI repository of machine learning databases, 1998. 88

[68] K. Nissim, S. Raskhodnikova, and A. Smith. Smooth sensitivity and sampling in private data analysis. In *Proceedings of the thirty-ninth annual ACM symposium on Theory of computing*, STOC '07, pages 75–84, New York, 2007. DOI: 10.1145/1250790.1250803. 70

[69] OECD. 2013 OECD Privacy Guidelines, 2013. http://www.oecd.org/internet/ie conomy/privacy-guidelines.htm 3

[70] A. Oganian and J. Domingo-Ferrer. On the complexity of optimal microaggregation for statistical disclosure control. *Statistical Journal of the United Nations Economic Comission for Europe*, 18(4):345–354, 2001. 20, 42

[71] D. Pedreschi, S. Ruggieri, and F. Turini. Discrimination-aware data mining. In *Proceedings of the 14th ACM SIGKDD International Conference on Knowledge Discovery and Data Mining*, pages 560–568, 2008. DOI: 10.1145/1401890.1401959. 107

[72] G. Pirró. A semantic similarity metric combining features and intrinsic information content. *Data Knowledge Engineering*, 68(11):1289–1308, November 2009. DOI: 10.1016/j.datak.2009.06.008. 93

[73] R. Rada, F. Mili, E. Bicknell, and M. Blettner. Development and application of a metric on semantic nets. *IEEE Transactions on Systems, Man and Cybernetics*, 19(1):17–30, 1989. DOI: 10.1109/21.24528. 93

[74] J. Reiter. Inference for partially synthetic, public use microdata sets. *Survey Methodology*, 9(2):181–188, 2003. 10, 21

[75] J. P. Reiter. Satisfying disclosure restrictions with synthetic datasets. *Journal of Official Statistics*, 18:531–544, 2002. 21

[76] M. Rodríguez-García, M. Batet, and D. Sánchez. Semantic noise: Privacy-protection of nominal microdata through uncorrelated noise addition. In *27th IEEE International Conference on Tools with Artificial Intelligence*, Vietri Sul Mare, Italy, 2015. 18

[77] D. B. Rubin. Discussion: statistical disclosure limitation. *Journal of Official Statistics*, 9:462–468, 1993. 9, 10, 21

[78] Y. Rubner, C. Tomasi, and L. J. Guibas. The earth mover's distance as a metric for image retrieval. *International Journal of Computer Vision*, 40(2):99–121, November 2000. DOI: 10.1023/A:1026543900054. 49

[79] P. Samarati. Protecting respondents' identities in microdata release. *IEEE Transactions on Knowledge and Data Engineering*, 13(6):1010–1027, November 2001. DOI: 10.1109/69.971193. 33, 38, 43

[80] P. Samarati and L. Sweeney. Protecting privacy when disclosing information: k-anonymity and its enforcement through generalization and suppression. Technical report, SRI International, 1998. 33, 43

[81] D. Sánchez and M. Batet. Semantic similarity estimation in the biomedical domain: an ontology-based information-theoretic perspective. *Journal of Biomedical Informatics*, 44(5):749–759, October 2011. DOI: 10.1016/j.jbi.2011.03.013. 93

[82] D. Sánchez and M. Batet. A new model to compute the information content of concepts from taxonomic knowledge. *International Journal on Semantic Web and Information Systems*, 8(2):34–50, 2012. DOI: 10.4018/jswis.2012040102. 93

[83] D. Sánchez and M. Batet. C-sanitized: a privacy model for document redaction and sanitization. *Journal of the Association for Information Science and Technology*, (to appear), 2015. DOI: 10.1002/asi.23363. 11

[84] D. Sánchez, M. Batet, D. Isern, and A. Valls. Ontology-based semantic similarity: a new feature-based approach. *Expert Systems With Applications*, 39(9):7718–7728, July 2012. DOI: 10.1016/j.eswa.2012.01.082. 89, 93, 94

[85] D. Sánchez, J. Domingo-Ferrer, and S. Martínez. Improving the utility of differential privacy via univariate microaggregation. In Josep Domingo-Ferrer, editor, *Privacy in Statistical Databases*, volume 8744 of *Lecture Notes in Computer Science*, pages 130–142. Springer International Publishing, 2014. DOI: 10.1007/978-3-642-15838-4. 77, 97

[86] D. Sánchez, J. Domingo-Ferrer, S. Martínez, and J. Soria-Comas. Utility-preserving differentially private data releases via individual ranking microaggregation. *Information Fusion*, 30:1–14, 2016. DOI: 10.1016/j.inffus.2015.11.002. 77, 97

[87] F. Sebé, J. Domingo-Ferrer, J. M. Mateo-Sanz, and V. Torra. Post-masking optimization of the tradeoff between information loss and disclosure risk in masked microdata sets. In Josep Domingo-Ferrer, editor, *Inference Control in Statistical Databases*, volume 2316 of *Lecture Notes in Computer Science*, pages 163–171. Springer Berlin Heidelberg, 2002. 11

[88] A. Solanas, A. Martínez-Ballesté, and J. Domingo-Ferrer. V-MDAV: a multivariate microaggregation with variable group size. In *Proceedings of COMPSTAT 2006*, August 2006. 54

[89] C. Song and T. Ge. Aroma: a new data protection method with differential privacy and accurate query answering. In *Proceedings of the 23rd ACM Conference on Information and Knowledge Management*, pages 1569–1578, 2014. DOI: 10.1145/2661829.2661886. 107

[90] J. Soria-Comas and J. Domingo-Ferrer. Probabilistic k-anonymity through microaggregation and data swapping. In *IEEE International Conference on Fuzzy Systems - FUZZ-IEEE 2012*, pages 1–8, 2012. DOI: 10.1109/FUZZ-IEEE.2012.6251280. 44

[91] J. Soria-Comas and J. Domingo-Ferrer. Differential privacy via t-closeness in data publishing. In *Eleventh Annual International Conference on Privacy, Security and Trust (PST)*, pages 27–35, July 2013. 73

[92] J. Soria-Comas and J. Domingo-Ferrer. Optimal data-independent noise for differential privacy. *Information Sciences*, 250:200–214, 2013. DOI: 10.1016/j.ins.2013.07.004. 18, 67

[93] J. Soria-Comas and J. Domingo-Ferrer. Big data privacy: challenges to privacy principles and models. *Data Science and Engineering*, pages 1–8, 2015. DOI: 10.1007/s41019-015-0001-x. 3, 106

[94] J. Soria-Comas and J. Domingo-Ferrer. Co-utile collaborative anonymization of microdata. In *Proceedings of MDAI 2015-Modeling Decisions for Artificial Intelligence*, pages 192–206. Springer, 2015. DOI: 10.1007/978-3-319-23240-9_16. 107

[95] J. Soria-Comas, J. Domingo-Ferrer, and D. Rebollo-Monedero. k-anonimato probabilístico. In *Actas de la XII Reunión Española sobre Criptología y Seguridad de la Información*, pages 249–254, Sep 2012. 44

[96] J. Soria-Comas, J. Domingo-Ferrer, D. Sánchez, and S. Martínez. Improving the utility of differentially private data releases via k-anonymity. In *12th IEEE International Conference on Trust, Security and Privacy in Computing and Communications (TrustCom)*, pages 372–379, July 2013. DOI: 10.1109/TrustCom.2013.47. 76, 79

[97] J. Soria-Comas, J. Domingo-Ferrer, D. Sánchez, and S. Martínez. Enhancing data utility in differential privacy via microaggregation-based k-anonymity. *The VLDB Journal*, 23(5):771–794, October 2014. DOI: 10.1007/s00778-014-0351-4. 51, 56, 76, 79

[98] J. Soria-Comas, J. Domingo-Ferrer, D. Sánchez, and S. Martínez. t-closeness through microaggregation: Strict privacy with enhanced utility preservation. *IEEE Transactions on Knowledge and Data Engineering*, 27(11):3098–3110, 2015. DOI: 10.1109/TKDE.2015.2435777. 53

[99] L. Sweeney. *Uniqueness of Simple Demographics in the U.S. Population*. LIDAP-WP4, Carnegie Mellon University, Laboratoty for International Data Privacy, Pittsburgh PA, 2000. 5

[100] L. Sweeney. k-Anonymity: a model for protecting privacy. *International Journal of Uncertainty, Fuzziness, and Knowledge-Based Systems*, 10(5):557–570, 2002. 32

[101] J. Terstegge. Privacy in the law. In M. Petkovic and W. Jonker, editors, *Security, Privacy, and Trust in Modern Data Management*, pages 11–20. Springer, 2007. DOI: 10.1007/978-3-540-69861-6. 3

[102] V. Torra and J. Domingo-Ferrer. Record linkage methods for multidatabase data mining. In V. Torra, editor, *Information Fusion in Data Mining*, pages 99–130. Springer, Berlin, 2003. DOI: 10.1007/978-3-540-36519-8. 29

[103] S. D. Warren and L. D. Brandeis. The right to privacy. *Harvard Law Review*, IV:193–220, 1890. DOI: 10.2307/1321160. 3

[104] L. Willenborg and T. DeWaal. *Elements of Statistical Disclosure Control*. Springer-Verlag, New York, 2001. DOI: 10.1007/978-1-4613-0121-9. 15

[105] M.-J. Woo, J.P. Reiter, A. Oganian, and A.F. Karr. Global measures of data utility for microdata masked for disclosure limitation. *Journal of Privacy and Confidentiality*, 1(1):111–124, 2009. 12

[106] Z. Wu and M. S. Palmer. Verb semantics and lexical selection. In J. Pustejovsky, editor, *Proceedings of the 32nd Annual Meeting on Association for Computational Linguistics*, pages 133–138. Morgan Kaufmann Publishers/ACL, 1994. 93

[107] X. Xiao and Y. Tao. Anatomy: simple and effective privacy preservation. In *Proceedings of the 32Nd International Conference on Very Large Data Bases*, VLDB '06, pages 139–150. VLDB Endowment, 2006. 44

[108] X. Xiao, G. Wang, and J. Gehrke. Differential privacy via wavelet transforms. *IEEE Transactions on Knowledge and Data Engineering*, 23(8):1200–1214, August 2011. DOI: 10.1109/TKDE.2010.247. 76

[109] Y. Xiao, L. Xiong, and C. Yuan. Differentially private data release through multidimensional partitioning. In Willem Jonker and Milan Petković, editors, *Secure Data Management*, volume 6358 of *Lecture Notes in Computer Science*, pages 150–168. Springer Berlin Heidelberg, 2010. 75

[110] J. Xu, Z. Zhang, X. Xiao, Y. Yang, and G. Yu. Differentially private histogram publication. In *Proceedings of the 28th IEEE International Conference on Data Engineering*, ICDE '12, pages 32–43, Washington, DC, 2012. IEEE Computer Society. DOI: 10.1007/s00778-013-0309-y. 75, 76

[111] J. Zhang, G. Cormode, C. M. Procopiuc, D. Srivastava, and X. Xiao. Privbayes: private data release via bayesian networks. In *Proceedings of the 2014 ACM SIGMOD International Conference on Management of Data*, SIGMOD '14, pages 1423–1434, New York, 2014. DOI: 10.1145/2588555.2588573. 76

Authors' Biographies

JOSEP DOMINGO-FERRER

Josep Domingo-Ferrer received an M.Sc. and a Ph.D. in computer science from the Autonomous University of Barcelona in 1988 and 1991, respectively. He also received an M.Sc. degree in mathematics. He is a Distinguished Professor of Computer Science and an ICREA-Acadèmia researcher at the Universitat Rovira i Virgili, Tarragona, Catalonia, where he holds the UNESCO Chair in Data Privacy. His research interests are in data privacy, data security, and cryptographic protocols. He is a Fellow of IEEE.

DAVID SÁNCHEZ

David Sánchez received a Ph.D. in computer science from the Technical University of Catalonia. He also received an M.Sc. degree in computer science from the Universitat Rovira i Virgili, Tarragona, Catalonia, in 2003, where he is currently an Associate Professor of Computer Science. His research interests are in data semantics and data privacy.

JORDI SORIA-COMAS

Jordi Soria-Comas received a B.Sc. degree in mathematics from the University of Barcelona in 2003, and an M.Sc. degree in finance from the Autonomous University of Barcelona in 2004. He received an M.Sc. degree in computer security in 2011, and a Ph.D. in computer science in 2013 from the Universitat Rovira i Virgili. He is a Director of Research at Universitat Rovira i Virgili. His research interests are in data privacy and security.

Printed in the United States
by Baker & Taylor Publisher Services